purple CHIPS

purple CHIPS

WINNING IN THE STOCK MARKET WITH THE VERY BEST OF THE BLUE CHIP STOCKS

JOHN SCHWINGHAMER

WILEY

John Wiley & Sons Canada, Ltd.

Library and Archives Canada Cataloguing in Publication Data

Schwinghamer, John

    Purple chips : winning in the stock market with the very best of the blue chip stocks / John Schwinghamer.

Includes index.
ISBN 978-11182-944-99

    1. Blue-chip stocks. 2. Investment analysis.
3. Corporations–Evaluation. 4. Investments–Psychological aspects. I. Title.

HG4661.S38 2012   332.63'22   C2012-901757-4

ISBN 978-1-118-29449-9 (pbk); 978-1-118-30009-1 (ebk);
978-1-118-30013-8 (ebk); 978-1-118-30014-5 (ebk)

Production Credits
Cover design and image: Ian Koo
Interior design: Adrian So
Typesetter: Laserwords
Printer: Trigraphik | LBF

John Wiley & Sons Canada, Ltd.
6045 Freemont Blvd.
Mississauga, Ontario
L5R 4J3

Printed in Canada

1 2 3 4 5 TRI 16 15 14 13 12

This book is dedicated to my wife, Jane, who has always been my best supporter and who still laughs at my jokes.

CONTENTS

Acknowledgments

I am grateful to the following people for their assistance in developing *Purple Chips*:

David Schwinghamer for his early guidance and editing skills; Raymond Kenworthy for all his research and analysis; Marilyn Biderman for sharing her vast knowledge of the publishing business; Mark Benthin for adding value; and Andre Bourret, Joseph Mendel and David Arthurs, for offering me their wisdom and support.

INTRODUCTION

With so many books on investing, you would be right to ask what could possibly make this one any better than what is already out there.

The answer is simple. I believe that if you take the time to read through the arguments that I put forward in this book, you will learn a simpler way to identify top-quality investments at good prices. If you follow the unique yet sensible approach that I propose in this book, your level of confidence will rise as you see yourself invest successfully, and with less risk, more often. This book will show you how to identify great companies based on a simple visual examination of their financial health. You will learn to invest with a well-defined plan that includes when to buy, when to sell and when to take a loss.

I wrote this book because through all my years in the financial industry, I have yet to come across a simple and effective way to invest. Most of the successful approaches I have seen involve extensive ratio analyses and screening procedures that are well beyond the practical ability and patience of most investors, and of many an investment advisor as well.

Many investors and professional advisors rely on analysts' reports rather than doing extensive analyses themselves. In my opinion, following analysts' reports is one of the more reliable ways to lose money or realize mediocre returns. Nowadays, due to the easy availability of information, the astute investor has access to tools and information that can easily replicate what the average professional advisor has to offer.

The methodology that I present starts with a strong foundation. It forces you to consider only the highest-quality companies and relies on long-term track records. The strength of this approach lies in its simplicity and effectiveness in identifying investment opportunities without having to do extensive financial analysis. The beauty of this approach is that it will identify the same investment opportunities that could otherwise be found only through extensive analysis.

The common wisdom seems to be that investing in the stock market is mastered only by going through the school of hard knocks, taking some finance courses and then investing, crossing your fingers and hoping that you don't get hurt too badly in the process. Failing that, you hope to be lucky enough to know a savvy investor who can help you navigate the ever-changing, turbulent seas of the stock market.

The alternative that you will learn about in this book is not earth-shattering; most astute investors would arrive at the same results. However, the approach that I take is a visual one: that is, one based on the consistent presentation—in graph form—of the same variables, which demonstrate the potential in any given stock. Once understood, the application of this analysis can save considerable time and effort and yield good results. It is also quite unlike the classic buy and hold strategy. It is simply a common sense approach that focuses on identifying the highest-quality companies at the right price. In short, this book will show you how to:

1. identify great companies;
2. buy their stocks when they are priced low;
3. sell them when they are priced high; and
4. repeat Steps 2 and 3 again and again.

Let's now take a quick look at my background and how I developed this approach.

My Background

I am a portfolio manager at a major bank in Montreal, Canada. I grew up in a middle-class family. My father was an engineer with more interest in the outdoors than in money, and my mother was a registered nurse who focused on savings. I was one of six children, and an average student in high school.

In my early adolescence I learned that I liked having money and that I liked making money. I started learning about investing when I bought my first motorcycle at the age of twelve. It was a Keystone 50cc two-stroke minibike, which was worth about $150. I rode it around for a year and then sold it for a profit. I traded up for a larger, more powerful off-road motorcycle, and then, with the passing seasons, another and another. At sixteen I moved on to cars. By the time I was twenty, I had bought and sold more than a dozen vehicles, and usually made a profit.

Those years taught me a fundamental lesson about making money: If you buy well, you can always sell at a profit. This lesson is what led to me becoming a value investor and developing a simple model that recognizes value.

My exposure to the stock market started when I was about eighteen and in college. In my student years, every summer I used to fly out to western Canada and work in the construction, oil and mining industries. After several summers, I had saved up enough money to start investing in stocks. I dabbled in the markets but soon realized that I could use some professional advice. I decided to find a savvy investment advisor who could teach me the ins and outs of the market.

Having no one to guide me on how to find an advisor, I presented myself at the reception desk of one of the major investment firms and asked for a meeting with a good broker. The receptionist politely invited me to have a seat and made a call. I spent a few minutes waiting anxiously in the reception area before a broker in his fifties emerged and greeted me. He looked a little uncomfortable, perhaps expecting someone older than my twenty-two years. Nonetheless, he seemed like a gentleman and I was excited to meet him. I eagerly answered his question about how much money I was looking to invest: $25,000— every penny I had. That amount sounded like a lot to me, but it did not impress him. He gently informed me that I didn't have enough capital to meet his minimum investment threshold. I was disappointed, but not for long, because he said he had a solution and then disappeared for a minute. When he came back, he was accompanied by Harry, a broker who not only looked slick to my eye, but as his business card told me, was a vice president. Wow, I thought. I can't go wrong with his advice.

I went so wrong. I came to learn that Harry's impressive title was not representative of his market prowess. It turned out that he was used to working with neophyte investors and was well aware that he could turn most of their investment capital into his own commissions. In other words, he would be pleased to take what I had and make it his. He sized me up as a rookie who knew little about investing and had the unrealistic, yet surprisingly pervasive, belief that doubling your money in a short time is possible. He saw me coming and changed my life.

This unscrupulous broker decided that I should place all of my capital in some gold mine warrants that would expire in about six weeks. He assured me that this was a surefire way to make a fast profit. Naively, I placed my trust and capital with him—the whole $25,000— which had taken me several summers to pull together and was every penny I had.

A few weeks later, I was stunned when the bad news came. I don't have the words to describe everything I felt. The warrants had gone to zero. I had lost everything. I was crushed, humiliated and more than a little upset.

Harry had taken me for a ride and, when he watched the warrants go to zero in a few short weeks, simply said to me, "Too bad, kid. It didn't work out." (While I was shattered at the time, it appears that what goes around comes around. Found guilty of having committed a number of frauds, Harry was barred from the securities industry in 2006.)

This experience traumatized me. It led to countless hours of thinking about what I could have done with all the money that I'd lost so easily. It gave me a burning desire to know why I had lost all the capital I had worked so hard to get. I was determined never to repeat that experience again.

In 1984, I graduated from university and was lucky enough to be hired in the Montreal Exchange's first-ever Apprentice Trader Program. The Exchange selected forty-five candidates to train in all areas of the investment industry, and to become licensed to work in various facets of the securities industry after the six-month intensive program. The program was the first of its kind and was expected to produce the next generation of investment-industry superstars. One of 1,500 applicants, I was fortunate enough to be among the select few who were accepted. I knew that if I could complete this program, I would find out why I had lost my $25,000, and would have the chance to become a successful and conscientious investment advisor to others.

Today, when I look back at the path I've taken, I realize that I turned a negative experience into a well-paid and satisfying career, into a job that makes work feel like play. I wrote this book because I discovered a better way to invest, and I think that if more investors were aware of this method, they might be able to avoid an experience like the one I had with an unscrupulous broker. The Purple Chips investment approach is an essential tool that should be part of every investor's toolbox.

The book is organized as follows: In Chapter 1 I discuss the psychology of investing and explain how the Purple Chips method fits in with human nature. In Chapter 2 we'll look more closely at Purple Chips stocks and why they are the most advantageous ones to own. In Chapters 3 and 4 I'll take you to the heart of my strategy, and examine the valuation of stocks and the phenomenon of valuation resets. Then I show you how to identify trends in valuation, and I discuss stock market crashes. In Chapter 5 I'll complete the picture by showing you how to buy and sell. In Chapter 6 we put them all to use with practice case studies so that you can see the Purple Chips method in action, and in Chapter 7 we conclude by bringing all of the concepts together.

CHAPTER 1

THE PSYCHOLOGY OF INVESTING

Human psychology is a key factor in investment strategy. As you know from the Introduction, I am not a psychologist, and I don't pretend to be one here. But what I have to say in this chapter is based on my experience as both an investor and a professional in the financial industry.

I believe that to become a successful long-term investor in the stock market, the best practice is to take smaller, continual rewards rather than the occasional big gain amidst a sea of disappointing misses. Regular success builds confidence, which is fundamental to becoming a good investor. Increased confidence allows you to think independently of the herd, and this mindset is essential to success.

Singles and Doubles Are Better

It's human nature to try to hit a home run, to want to experience the glory and praise that come from knocking the ball out of the park. We yearn to be singled out as the person who has achieved something exceptional. The problem with this strategy is that, in the world of investing, more often than not you'll miss. While you may have the occasional success, over time you are likely to lose your bravado, and fall into an inevitable slump as you wait for your next home run.

Most people don't react well to failure, whether it is the occasional big one or frequent little ones. If you're looking for home runs, you will fail most of the time. The following example illustrates how the human psyche deals with success and failure.

Imagine a game show that presents you with two choices: Door Number 1 and Door Number 2.

The show's host calls you down from the audience and explains the game. "Okay, John, here's how we play this game. I give you $1,000 and you choose either Door Number 1 or Door Number 2. Then I will ask you to decide if you want to continue with your prize or stop playing. You'll have a choice to make, you can walk away at any time."

"All right," you say, "let's go with Door Number 1."

Door Number 1 opens wide to reveal four suitcases, one of which you must pick. You make your choice, the host opens it and you've just lost $300. You have $700 left.

"Pick another one, John. We're not done yet." You choose again, and again you lose some money, this time $200. You're left with $500, which is half of what you started with, and two remaining suitcases.

The host says to you, "So, John, my friend, would you like to continue or do you want to play it safe and keep what you have?" You reflect on the fact that you began with $1,000, dropped first to $700 and then to $500. Most people, in my experience, would be inclined to call it quits at this point—which in my industry means either changing investment advisors or dropping out of investing in the stock market altogether.

This is human nature and nothing to be ashamed of, as far as I'm concerned. We're all drawn to quick returns and always hope to hit that glorious home run, and if neither comes quickly, we look elsewhere to find that positive experience.

Imagine now that, just for fun, the host opens the last two suitcases. It turns out that one of them held yet another loss of $200, but the final suitcase held a gain of $1,700, our elusive home run. Had you followed through and opened all of the suitcases, you would have gained $1,000, and wound up with $2,000 in the end.

Now let's imagine a different course of events. After the host gives you his spiel and the $1,000, you pick Door Number 2, which, as it turns out, presents you with a different scenario. With your first choice of suitcase, you've won $200. The host asks if you want to continue and, of course, you do. "I've just won $200. I've still got my original $1,000. Let's go."

Much to your delight, although it would be nice if the amount were larger, the next suitcase gives you a gain of another $100. "You're on a roll," the host says. "What do you say?"

And with the next suitcase you win another $400, and you're sitting on $1,700 in total. There is one suitcase left and you go for it, and, wonder of wonders, you win another $300 and finish the game with $2,000. Most people would agree that the scenario behind Door Number 2 is a far more attractive one. It's certainly less dramatic, but far easier on the nerves, and one that most people would be far more likely to see through to its conclusion.

The second scenario in this game-show analogy illustrates the psychology of my method of investing in the stock market. I recognize that positive reinforcement helps an investor build confidence, and the approach that I propose in this book is based on incremental success, on strings of singles and doubles, rather than the odd home run. I will show you how to invest in order to realize a high frequency of small- and medium-sized gains. The key is to find companies with long-term upward trends in their stocks' earnings per share (EPS). EPS is a key concept in my method and I will explain it in further detail in the next chapter.

This approach is not as glamorous as a home run, but a steady succession of small to medium gains will give you a better chance of sticking to a plan than will several losses followed by a large gain.

Only an investor with an iron stomach, or a gambler's unfailing faith in his luck, would see the first game-show scenario to its conclusion. This point is so important that it bears repeating: *The second scenario builds confidence, which helps investors see a plan through to its conclusion, which in turn makes for a better and more successful investor.*

Tune Out the Noise

We've just seen the value of going for singles and doubles rather than home runs. Another significant part of this approach involves tuning out the noise. "Noise" is my term for all the news and events that occur in the stock market after you invest. These bits of information, which may be inaccurate and speculative, are distractions that will keep you from reaching your goal. They eat away at your confidence, leading you to doubt your original plan.

As investors, one of the hardest things to overcome is our emotions. It takes enormous discipline to develop a plan, avoid distractions and follow the plan to completion. When you think of placing your capital in an investment, you usually have buy and sell targets in mind, as well as a time frame. Then you are distracted by the noise and you're led astray.

For example, imagine that you bought shares of Johnson & Johnson at a low valuation (i.e., underpriced in light of their potential to increase in value), but then a short time later you read that several analysts are expecting a correction, a general downward trend, in the stock market. Hearing this news from "the experts" could lead you to sell your Johnson & Johnson shares for fear of a decline in stock price. If you are susceptible to noise, your exposure to the analysts' predictions may cause you to change your plan.

What separates truly gifted investors from average ones is their level of discipline. A superior investor follows a plan and has the confidence to ignore the noise and distractions that could otherwise disrupt the plan.

Consider the following. Most investors who own a house are disciplined investors. There are at least two reasons for this:

1. They need a place to live and they have no intention of selling their home.
2. They are not aware of the changing value of their investment in their home.

Imagine if all houses had electronic billboards attached to their fronts so that homeowners could see the changing value of their houses every day. If a house price moved like a typical stock, then it would not be uncommon for a $300,000 house to go up or down by 1%, or $3,000, in a day. For many people, this would probably be equivalent to the cost of a week-long vacation in a nice place. Most people would be unnerved knowing that on any given day they had just made or lost the equivalent of a nice holiday. Because homeowners don't see the changing daily values of their houses, they are much less affected by these changes, and so follow their plan to stay where they are, unaffected by fluctuations in value.

If homeowners knew that their houses were going up or down by large amounts, there would be more trading, and less long-term investing, in houses than there currently is. A disciplined investor, like most homeowners, has a plan and sticks to it, knowing full well that there will be ups and downs on the way to reaching the long-term goal of seeing an investment strategy through to completion.

Discipline in investing means being able to follow a plan and avoiding all the obstacles and distractions that the market will place in your way.

EPS Explained

Let's now take a more concrete look at singles and doubles using the Purple Chips approach.

In the following exhibits, I refer to C.R. Bard, which trades under the stock symbol "BCR" on the New York Stock Exchange (NYSE).

Exhibit 1.1 Calculating EPS

Date	Quarter	Earnings per share (EPS)	Trailing 12-month EPS
Dec. 2010	Q4	$1.54	$5.61
Sept. 2010	Q3	$1.43	$5.46
June 2010	Q2	$1.39	n/a
Mar. 2010	Q1	$1.25	n/a
Dec. 2009	Q4	$1.39	n/a

C.R. Bard is a large American maker of medical devices that are used in hospitals around the world. Before I go into details, we need to understand the concept of "earnings per share," because it is the foundation of the Purple Chips method. EPS is simply a measure of how much money a company has earned in its most recent four quarters, or one-year period, for every share that is owned by shareholders.

Exhibit 1.1 shows the EPS for C.R. Bard from December (Q4) 2009 to December (Q4) 2010. If we add up the four quarters of EPS in 2010, we get what is referred to as the trailing twelve-month EPS of $5.61 per share for the one-year period ending December 2010 ($5.61 = $1.54 + $1.43 + $1.39 + $1.25). Note that the trailing twelve-month EPS is sometimes also referred to as the rolling twelve-month EPS. For the purposes of this book we will use only the former term, which is abbreviated as TTM. So, in September 2010 (Q3), the trailing EPS was $5.46, which is the sum of Q3 2010, Q2 2010, Q1 2010 and Q4 2009 (the last four quarters).

If we were to record a trailing twelve-month EPS for each quarter on a time chart, we end up with the EPS line that you will see in most of the exhibits in this book.

Exhibit 1.2 shows the layout of the chart used throughout this book. The top line of the chart shows us information such as the chart type, trading symbol, name of share issuer, last sale price, change from the previous close, TTM earnings per share and the price/earnings multiple (note that the term "price/earnings multiple"

Exhibit 1.2   C.R. Bard (BCR, May 2011)

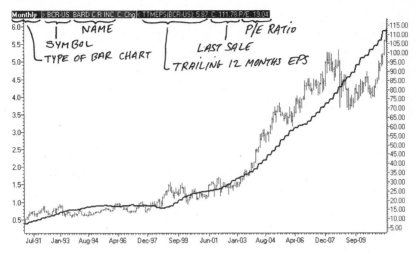

and "price/earnings ratio" are interchangeable, but for clarity, we will use "multiple").

Exhibit 1.3 gives definitions of the remaining information on the chart. On the bottom of the graph you'll see time marked out in intervals where each tick represents one month, and on the left side,

Exhibit 1.3   Understanding the Scales—C.R. Bard (BCR, May 2011)

the EPS scale, which shows the EPS in dollars. On the right side, the scale shows the stock price in dollars. The stock price is presented as a series of vertical bars, with each bar representing the trading range for one month. The heavy black line shows the EPS at a certain date. Note that the EPS line in every chart in this book ends at that last trade price of the stock. As you will see later, the position of the EPS line on the stock chart allows you to see changes in valuation that will highlight investment opportunities.

The EPS line differs from the stock bars because it appears as a series of steps. When you display these factors together in this visual form, you can see that the EPS line is much less volatile than the stock price. That is to say that the EPS line is steady and moves in a predictable fashion, whereas the stock price seems to move in a wild and unpredictable manner. As you read this book it will become obvious to you that unlike a stock price, the earnings or EPS of a company are not influenced by emotions.

Exhibit 1.4 charts the stock price of C.R. Bard with its EPS. The point at which the two dashed lines intersect shows that the EPS was $5.61 per share in December 2010.

Exhibit 1.4 Reading the EPS—C.R. Bard (BCR, May 2011)

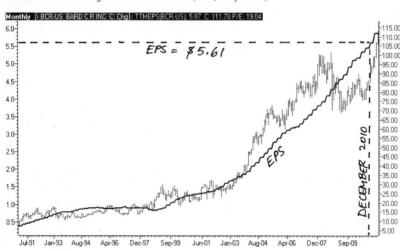

Exhibit 1.5 Abbott Labs (ABT, August 2011)

Exhibit 1.5 demonstrates how the Purple Chips model would have[1] bought and sold the stock of Abbott Labs (ABT) between the years 1999 and 2011. "B" and "S" mark the buy and sell points over the years. Using this approach, the result is a gross profit of $24.40 per share. This is not bad considering that while an investor was not invested in Abbott Labs, he could have been putting his capital to work in other opportunities that were highlighted by the Purple Chips approach. Therefore he could maximize the use of his capital. Chapter 6 details Abbott Labs in a case study.

Exhibit 1.6 shows the results of the buying and selling of Abbott Labs in tabular form.

Exhibit 1.6 Gain/Loss Summary for Abbott Labs

Date	Buy	Date	Sell	Gain/Loss
Dec. 1999	$33.10	May 2000	$38.90	$ 5.80
June 2002	$37.10	July 2002	$37.10	$ 0.00
Feb. 2003	$34.10	May 2003	$40.90	$ 6.80
Nov. 2005	$40.10	Jan. 2007	$51.90	$11.80
Oct. 2008	$51.10	Oct. 2009	$51.10	$ 0.00
June 2010	$46.10	-	-	-
			Total gain/loss	$24.40

The preceding example with Abbott Labs demonstrates that this methodology *is based on finding good-quality companies, buying them when they are inexpensive and selling them when they are expensive.* In more technical terms, we buy the stocks of top-quality companies when their valuation is low and the odds favor a return to a more reasonable valuation. We hold on to these stocks until their valuation has risen to the point at which we have determined it is advantageous to sell, and then repeat the process, buying and selling the same good company whenever we identify investment opportunities.

Of course, we don't rely on just one or even a very small number of companies. The success of this model is based on identifying a select, but reasonably sized, group of companies and waiting for each of these candidates to become a bargain.

CHAPTER 2

PURPLE CHIPS VERSUS BLUE CHIPS

At the end of Chapter 1, I said that "Purple Chips is based on finding good quality companies, buying them when they are inexpensive and selling them when they are expensive." In this chapter, we will focus on the first part of that sentiment: the criteria that guide our choice of companies to invest in. They are the criteria that define a Purple Chip company and provide the underlying strength that makes the Purple Chips model a lower-risk approach to investing. As we examine these criteria for several companies, it will also become clear that the innovative visual approach of this model is faster and more effective than using the traditional method of examining companies by looking at their financial ratios. Financial ratios are the yardstick most commonly used to compare similar companies; there are ratios for every financial aspect of a company, which serve to highlight their strengths and weaknesses.

Finding the Purple Chips

"Purple Chips" is the term that I use to describe the stocks of companies that meet the Purple Chips model's selection criteria. These criteria differentiate our investment candidates from ordinary blue chip stocks. Purple Chips are the royalty of blue chips. They are the highest level of quality in the stock hierarchy.

There are three main criteria for a company to qualify as a Purple Chip. Companies must have:

1. a minimum seven years of positive and growing EPS;
2. smooth and predictable growth in EPS; and
3. a minimum market capitalization of $1 billion.

Minimum Seven Years of Positive and Growing EPS

The first criterion is that a Purple Chip stock must have exhibited growth in EPS for a minimum of seven years.

To ensure that companies report their earnings in a consistent and comparable manner, Generally Accepted Accounting Principles require every public company to report its earnings in a consistent manner and on a quarterly basis; in other words, once every three months.

Over the past decade, there has been a trend among investors to focus on short-term considerations at the expense of long-term ones. I believe that this trend has been fueled by faster business cycles and the fact that companies have to be quick and nimble to succeed in this ever-changing environment. While the climate has changed for many industries and the flow of information and goods is much faster than it used to be, the investment strategy proposed here runs counter to this ideology. The Purple Chips model is based on the belief that a long-term track record speaks volumes about how a company deals with the challenges of everyday business. The very best companies are those that consistently outperform competitors over the long term, and also exhibit certain hallmarks in the smoothness and predictability of their EPS over an extended period of time.

I feel that I need a minimum of seven years of historical earnings data to satisfy the criterion of the long-term perspective of the Purple Chips method. I chose this period because, in most cases, the management of a company cannot obscure or manipulate the company's true performance over such a long time frame. Remember Bre-X or Enron or WorldCom? These companies did not have the benefit of a long history of earnings, and investors soon discovered that the reported earnings were fictitious. Also, during a seven-year period most companies will have gone through sector-specific challenges or business cycles, which are the real test for any business. For example, a company can experience a business challenge that will have a marked impact on its earnings, but the truly outstanding company will rise above the challenge and find new ways of growing its earnings. And a look at its seven-year earnings will amply demonstrate this strength.

Smooth and Predictable Growth in EPS

The second criterion that defines a Purple Chip stock is a smooth and predictable earnings history. Earnings are the primary driver of stock prices. When earnings rise, stock prices usually follow. When they drop, so do stock prices. Because stock prices are driven by earnings, a company's earnings history provides key information in determining when a stock is good value and when it isn't. The following analogy illustrates the behavior of stock prices relative to a company's earnings. Exhibit 2.1 shows a large ocean liner cruising through the sea with a small rowboat tethered to it. As the ocean liner moves through the water it pulls the rowboat, which weaves from side to side but never strays too far from the big boat, thanks to its tether. Where the big boat goes, the small boat follows. While the ocean liner follows a steady and predictable path, however, the rowboat follows an erratic path, oscillating from side to side in the larger boat's wake. The rowboat gets pushed around by wind, waves and other factors that do not change the path of the ocean liner.

Now picture a bar chart of a company's share price that shows the stock price and the EPS over a long period of time. They behave just as

Exhibit 2.1 Ocean Liner Pulling Rowboat

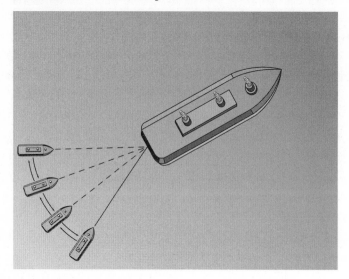

the two boats do: the ocean liner's path is analogous to that of the EPS and the tethered boat's path is analogous to the stock price.

Exhibit 2.2 shows a bar chart of International Business Machines' (IBM) stock price and EPS line over twenty years. Note the steady EPS line and the erratic behavior of the stock price.

Exhibit 2.2 International Business Machines (IBM, May 2011)

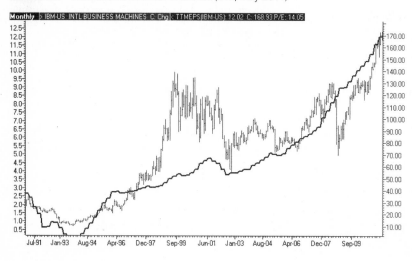

Notice that the graph of the stock earnings, or EPS line, is a relatively straight line and the line for stock price is more erratic, with more dramatic ups and downs. So, the visual element of the Purple Chips method clearly shows the stock earnings line as the ocean liner and the stock price as the rowboat that is tethered to it. Where the big boat goes, the small boat follows; or where the earnings go, the price eventually follows. This is an important concept to grasp: *Earnings tell you where a stock's price is going in the future, which helps you gauge the stock's current value.* When the ocean liner begins to make what appears to be a slow, calculated turn, the rowboat will always follow. Exhibit 2.3 shows the EPS and stock price lines for Whole Foods Market (WFM), a U.S.-based chain of supermarkets that specializes in natural and organic foods. Until 2006, the company's stock had performed well, as Purple Chips stocks do. Then their earnings began to deteriorate, and Whole Foods' stock price quickly followed the downward shift in earnings.

Every once in a while, the market forgets that earnings are the first place to look when seeking value. Recall the 1999 to 2000 dotcom craze when all things Internet were going public and stock prices were stratospheric. In many cases, first-day gains on an Initial Public

Exhibit 2.3   Whole Foods Market (WFM, May 2011)

Offering (IPO) were staggering, with some IPOs registering 50% gains on their first day of trading. The following excerpt and headlines were typical of IPOs in 1999:

> "Shooting out of the gate this morning, iVillage ran up nearly 300 percent on its first trade, as the women's network became the latest Internet company to join the public market."
> *Dawn Kawamoto, "iVillage Hits the Roof on Its Debut," CNET News, March 19, 1999, http://news.cnet.com/2100-1023-223271 .html&pt.salon.*

> "IPO Roundup: Internet Capital Group Flies in Debut, Mission Critical Also Gains"
> *Tiffany Kary, CNET News, August 5, 1999, http://news.cnet .com/IPO-Roundup-Internet-Capital-Group-flies-in-debut, -Mission-Critical-also-gains/2100-12_3-265295.html.*

> "Marketwatch.com IPO Stuns the Street"
> *Dawn Kawamoto, CNET News, January 15, 1999, http://news .cnet.com/Marketwatch.com-IPO-stuns-the-Street/2100-1023_ 3-220222.html.*

These staggeringly large gains were fueled by the belief at the time that the stock market was entering a new era, and that valuations should no longer be measured by profitability. Many Internet companies had disclaimers in their prospectuses stating that their business model could not be expected to generate any foreseeable earnings. Incredibly, many investors continued to buy these overvalued experiments. This was the new economy and investors had begun to believe that the "old" valuation models were no longer applicable. As we know, this experiment ended badly. Many investors lost a great deal of money. Had they paid attention to valuation models, they could have avoided the devastating losses they suffered. Had they followed a plan that told them to consider only stocks with seven years' worth of stable and predictable earnings—the foundation of value—they would not have lost their money. Investors who follow the Purple Chips model, however, will not fall into this trap. They will be buying reliable, quality stocks at an attractive price.

Minimum Market Capitalization of $1 Billion

Another criterion that defines a company whose stocks are Purple Chips is its size. I insist on considering only companies with a market capitalization of $1 billion or more. Market capitalization is defined as the total value of the company. This is the stock price multiplied by every outstanding share in the company. For example, if ABC Company has 1 million shares outstanding and its shares trade at $10 per share, then:

$$\text{ABC Market Capitalization} = 1{,}000{,}000 \text{ shares} \times \$10 \text{ per share}$$
$$\text{Market Capitalization} = \$10{,}000{,}000$$

To understand why size matters, we'll now compare ocean liners to speedboats.

Ocean liners require the input of dozens of people to operate properly and they're made to withstand rough seas with thirty-foot waves. Both of these elements contribute to their stability. They may not move fast, but their actions are steady and, most of all, predictable.

Conversely, a speedboat, with its single driver and perhaps a few passengers, accelerates quickly and can zip from side to side in a fraction of the time that an ocean liner requires. It cannot, however, withstand the crush of a thirty-foot wave.

Now consider a young company that is run like a speedboat. It has a small market capitalization, it is guided by a smaller management team and its movements are far less predictable. With its smaller foothold in the marketplace, it is also far more susceptible to the ravages of sudden changes in market forces, such as, for example, the sudden arrival of a major competitor (a thirty-foot wave), which until now had ignored the small company's niche market. While there are great investment opportunities in companies with small capitalization, the Purple Chips method requires that earnings are predictable, and it is therefore not suitable to apply it to start-ups and other companies in their infancy.

Our focus is ocean liners. These companies have a market capitalization of $1 billion or more. They offer a less thrilling ride but they produce steady and predictable earnings that yield a predictable price action from which we can profit. Their predictability is what creates our investment opportunity.

Purple Chips versus Common Blue Chips

Be careful, however, not to confuse the size of a company with its level of quality. "Blue chip" used to be synonymous with a good-quality stock that paid a healthy dividend—the kind of stock that your banker or wealthy friend owned. A blue chip stock was a stock that you were unlikely to lose money on: all you had to do was wait for the eventual appreciation in its stock price. Nowadays, the moniker "blue chip" is applied to just about any large company that becomes a household name. "Blue chip" has become an unreliable description because many large companies that carry this label do not have the hallmarks of a real blue chip. The easiest way to spot the imposters is to examine the smoothness and predictability of their earnings.

Before we look at the imposters, let's look at a company that most would agree is not in the blue chip or Purple Chips category: Electronic Arts (ERTS). Electronic Arts develops and markets video games that are found in many American homes. I like this example because it illustrates how important stable and predictable earnings are if you are trying to figure out what a company is worth. Exhibit 2.4 is the graph for Electronic Arts from 1991 to 2011. Note how the earnings fluctuate wildly over the years. At times they appear to be steady, and then suddenly they rise or fall sharply. Although the stock price generally follows the trend in earnings, the earnings are so volatile that they cannot be easily predicted. In this circumstance it is nearly impossible to know when the stock represents good value.

Now let's move on to the imposters of the blue chip world. Ford (F), DuPont and Verizon have all been called blue chip at some point in time but none of them produce the smooth and predictable earnings

Exhibit 2.4   Electronic Arts (ERTS, June 2011)

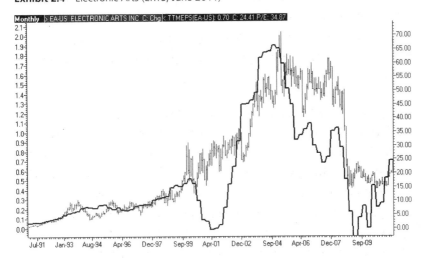

that are typical of real blue chips. This is why I coined the term "Purple Chips." Purple Chips are the real blue chips, the royalty of blue chips. Look at exhibit 2.5, which graphically demonstrates the volatile earnings of Ford, a so-called blue chip company. Its earnings swing so wildly as to defy predictability. In this case, the extreme levels of the EPS line were literally off the chart!

Exhibit 2.5   Ford (F, May 2011)

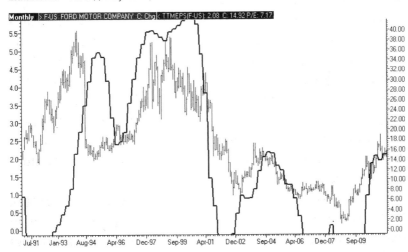

Volatile earnings make it hard to know what a stock should be worth, and therefore when to buy it. In the Purple Chips model, we focus only on companies that have stable and predictable earnings. These characteristics help us to determine when the price of a stock is at an unreasonably low level. We know that there is a high probability that the stock will revert back up to its average price or, to put it more technically, the statistical norm or mean price. A visual analysis of the earnings gives us the ability to buy with confidence because that picture of a Purple Chip stock tells us what we need to know. The earnings are continuing on a path that will eventually pull the stock price up, just like the ocean liner with the rowboat in tow.

DuPont and Verizon are also companies whose stocks are widely held and are often referred to as blue chip stocks. At one time they may have had the characteristics of a classic blue chip, but they are no longer in the same league as the Purple Chip companies that we are looking for.

Exhibit 2.6 shows how the earnings of DuPont (DD) have been anything but predictable. Consequently, the stock price has followed the vagaries of its earnings path.

Exhibit 2.6 DuPont (DD, May 2011)

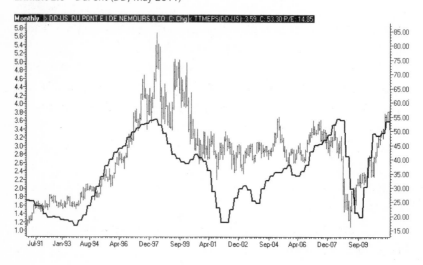

Exhibit 2.7   Verizon (VZ, May 2011)

Exhibit 2.7 shows that the earnings of Verizon (VZ) have not been too volatile but have been on a steady downward path since 2001. Not surprisingly, the shares have followed the same path.

A Purple Chip's most important hallmark is steady and predictable growth in earnings over a long period of time. We can see its signature smooth ascending pattern on the graphs. That smooth and rising EPS line is your assurance that, most of the time, if you buy at a low valuation as defined by the Purple Chips method, you have a good chance of making money.

Exhibit 2.8 is the chart of Abbott Labs for the last twenty years. Note the smooth ascending slope of the EPS line. This is what a Purple Chip looks like. Steady and predictable earnings, no surprises.

Wal-Mart (WMT) is another fine example of a Purple Chip (see exhibit 2.9). In this case, the chart shows that earnings were less than $0.40 per share in 1991 but grew steadily to around $4.18 per share by mid-2011.

Note how exhibits 2.8 and 2.9 show steady and predictable growth in earnings—*for twenty years.*

Exhibit 2.8 Smooth EPS—Abbott Labs (ABT, May 2011)

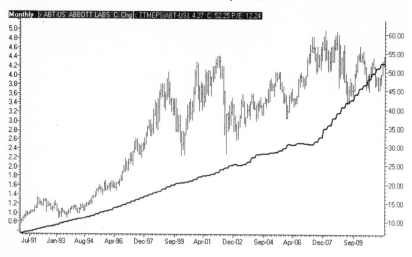

Exhibit 2.9 Wal-Mart (WMT, May 2011)

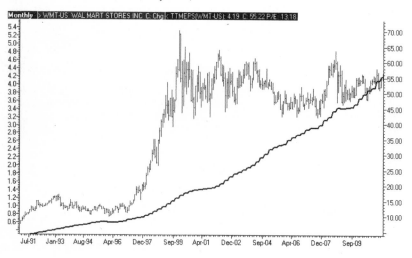

Dilution Is a Value Killer

The EPS lines for Abbott and Wal-Mart bring up another important characteristic of the Purple Chips model. The EPS lines show how profits are affected by dilution. Dilution occurs when a company reports increasing profits in dollar terms, but the benefit of the increased

Exhibit 2.10   WaterDown Inc. Earnings

Year	Earnings	Shares outstanding	EPS
2005	$10,000,000	20,000,000	$0.50
2006	$15,000,000	25,000,000	$0.60
2007	$17,000,000	30,000,000	$0.57
2008	$18,000,000	40,000,000	$0.45

dollar profit is offset by a higher number of shares. To a shareholder, dilution is a value killer. In exhibits 2.10 through 2.13 we show how dilution can affect the EPS of two companies, WaterDown Inc. and MoneyMaker Inc.

Exhibit 2.10 shows that from 2005 to 2008, WaterDown has increased its total earnings from $10 million to $18 million, but on a per share basis, its EPS has declined over the four-year time frame, because it issued twenty million new shares. We can see the effect of dilution in exhibit 2.11 when the EPS line begins to decline because the earnings have been divided amongst a larger number of shares.

Compare this to MoneyMaker Inc. in exhibit 2.12, which made the same dollar amount in earnings but did not issue any new shares. Here you see how the EPS has grown because there has not been any shareholder dilution.

Exhibit 2.11   WaterDown Inc. EPS

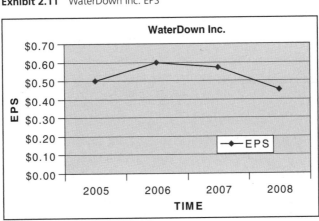

Exhibit 2.12 MoneyMaker Inc. Earnings

Year	Earnings	Shares outstanding	EPS
2005	$10,000,000	20,000,000	$0.50
2006	$15,000,000	20,000,000	$0.75
2007	$17,000,000	20,000,000	$0.85
2008	$18,000,000	20,000,000	$0.90

Exhibit 2.13 MoneyMaker Inc. EPS

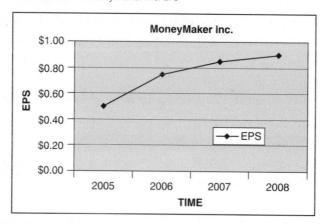

The upward slope of MoneyMaker's EPS line in exhibit 2.13 means that MoneyMaker is the superior investment when compared to WaterDown. The stockholders of WaterDown saw their holdings diluted by 50% due to their company's prolific issuance of new shares. This chart illustrates how important the EPS line is to shareholders, because it takes into account the effect of shareholder dilution and can be used as a comprehensive gauge of a company's health.

After examining all of these different graphs, you can see that the EPS line is the predominant factor in determining the direction of a stock price. If the earnings of a company are steady and predictable, it follows that the price of its stock can be easily predicted. If the earnings of a company are erratic and unpredictable, it's more difficult to predict the price of its stock.

In conclusion, we can say that the companies we are looking for all have the same characteristics. They have a long history of steady, predictable and rising earnings. We know that earnings per share are the number one driver of the stock price of any large company, and so the companies that demonstrate that trait are the ones we look for. The steady, rising trend of the EPS line is what gives us the confidence to buy the shares when they are at a low valuation.

Dividends, or Getting Paid While You Wait

The Purple Chips method focuses on the best companies in a sector, and will typically lead to companies that pay dividends. This comes as no surprise since the companies that pay dividends are usually the same ones that have predictable cash flow and superior track records. Investors like dividends because they get paid while they wait for their stocks to appreciate.

Another reason that investors favor companies that pay dividends is because a large part of the return that investors have made in the stock market has come from dividends. Some companies pay dividends to shareholders as an incentive to own their shares. A company usually declares a dividend when it has a reliable stream of income that comes from a history of predictable profits or EPS. Dividends are paid to shareholders on a quarterly basis. According to Ibbotson Associates, from 1926 to 2005, over 40% of the total return from stocks came from dividends.[1] Ned Davis Research corroborates this fact, stating that dividend-paying stocks outperformed non-dividend paying stocks by 7% per year based on the historical returns of the S&P 500 from 1972 to 2009.[2] This trend should not come as a surprise. Another incentive for owning dividend-paying stocks is that their prices tend to be more stable than their non-dividend paying counterparts.

Purple Chips Make Money for Investors

At this point, you have learned how to identify a Purple Chip and should be able to see the benefits of buying the best companies that are available to investors. Now I will give you another reason as to why this approach should appeal to you. The list in exhibit 2.16 comprises the top Purple Chips on U.S. stock exchanges as of July 7, 2011. (Note that the list of Purple Chip candidates does change slightly over time and this date was chosen as a reference point to illustrate how this approach performed; any date could have been chosen after the crash of 2008 to reach my conclusion).

These companies all meet the basic Purple Chip criteria:

1. a minimum seven years of positive and growing EPS;
2. smooth and predictable growth in EPS; and
3. a minimum market capitalization of $1 billion.

There are approximately 250 companies listed on the U.S. stock exchanges that meet the criteria of the Purple Chips model.[3] The addition of one criterion, however, will eliminate all but twenty-five companies. These twenty-five companies are the top ones out of the population of 250 Purple Chips as demonstrated by the smoothness of their EPS lines. Since 2003, these companies have had the lowest volatility in their EPS and have had very few quarters of declining EPS. In other words, their EPS continued in an upward trend with very little interruption. Conversely, their peers experienced noticeable declines during the credit crisis of 2008 and 2009 due to the substantial slow-down of the American economy.

See exhibits 2.14 and 2.15 for examples of the high prices used in this example for Hewlett Packard (HPQ) and Oracle (ORCL) prior to the crash of 2008. These charts show the worst price prior to the crash of 2008. This exercise implies that you would have invested in these top Purple Chips at very high prices. In reality, this approach would never suggest that you invest at the worst price; however, as you will see, it demonstrates the superior quality of this group of stocks.

The conclusion of this exercise is the following: Remarkably, if an investor had bought these twenty-five companies in equal weights (4% each = 25 × 4% = 100%) at the highest (and worst possible) price prior to the stock market crash of late 2008 and 2009, the investor would have made a return of approximately 8% on his portfolio of twenty-five stocks. Compare this to the return of negative 14% for the S&P 500 Index if you had bought the component stocks of this index when it was at its highest price of $1,576.09 prior to the crash of 2008 and 2009, and calculated your return as of July 7, 2011, when the Index was $1,353.22. The S&P 500 Index is a broad index of 500 stocks that most investors and fund managers use to compare to their own performance. If you

Exhibit 2.14 Hewlett Packard (HPQ, July 2011)

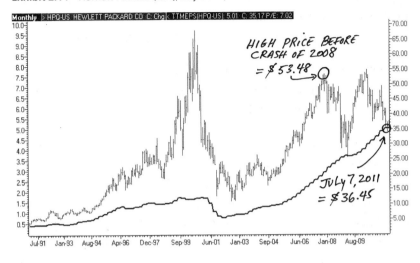

Exhibit 2.15 Oracle (ORCL, July 2011)

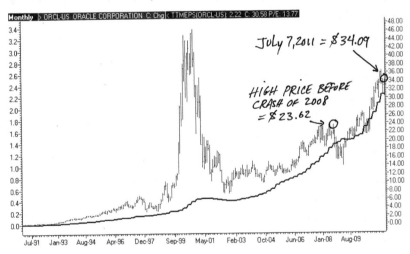

can beat the S&P 500 you are usually considered to be an outstanding investor. Recall also that the Purple Chips approach does not advise you to buy when valuations are high, so it is reasonable to assume that had you followed the Purple Chips model, the entry points would have been more favorable than if you had bought at the worst possible price prior to the crash.

The above example should cause you to ask yourself why anyone would invest in a company that is not a Purple Chip. If you want to

Exhibit 2.16 Top Purple Chips

	Symbol	Industry	High price before crash	Price on July 7, 2011	% Change
HEWLETT PACKARD	HPQ	Computer Hardware	$ 53.48	$ 36.45	−32%
EMC	EMC	Computer Hardware	$ 25.47	$ 27.89	10%
MCCORMICK	MKC	Food Processing	$ 42.06	$ 49.94	19%
SJ SMUCKER	SJM	Food Processing	$ 64.32	$ 77.08	20%
FLOWERS FOODS	FLO	Food Processing	$ 21.79	$ 22.91	5%
FRESENIUS	FMS	Healthcare	$ 59.11	$ 74.74	26%
EXPRESS SCRIPTS	ESRX	Healthcare	$ 39.55	$ 54.83	39%
ECOLAB	ECL	Household Products	$ 52.78	$ 56.64	7%
CHURCH & DWIGHT	CHD	Household Products	$ 32.77	$ 41.10	25%
TEVA	TEVA	Pharma	$ 50.00	$ 49.34	−1%
MCDONALD'S	MCD	Restaurants	$ 67.00	$ 86.06	28%
ORACLE	ORCL	Software	$ 23.62	$ 34.09	44%
MEDCO HEALTH SOLN	MHS	Healthcare	$ 54.63	$ 55.86	2%
DAVITA	DVA	Healthcare	$ 67.44	$ 89.36	33%
MEDNAX	MD	Healthcare	$ 72.51	$ 73.64	2%
AFLAC	AFL	Insurance Health	$ 68.81	$ 47.40	−31%
IBM	IBM	IT Services	$ 130.93	$ 176.48	35%
DST SYSTEMS	DST	IT Services	$ 82.35	$ 55.24	−33%
MEDTRONIC	MDT	Med. Equip & Supplies	$ 62.00	$ 38.20	−38%
BECTON DICKINSON	BDX	Med. Equip & Supplies	$ 93.24	$ 89.74	−4%
C.R. BARD	BCR	Med. Equip & Supplies	$ 101.61	$ 113.32	12%
JOHNSON & JOHNSON	JNJ	Pharma	$ 72.76	$ 67.92	−7%
ABBOTT LABS	ABT	Pharma	$ 61.09	$ 53.54	−12%
WALMART	WMT	Retail	$ 70.25	$ 54.49	−22%
FACTSET	FDS	Investment Services	$ 66.40	$ 102.91	55%
				Purple Chips weighted return	**8%**
		S&P500	$1,576.09	$1,353.22	**−14%**

make money in the stock market, stick to the best and buy quality. Buy Purple Chips.

Keeping It Simple: The Purple Chips Model versus Ratio Analysis

In this section, I will prove that the visual approach of Purple Chips is a simpler and faster way to analyze companies than is conventional ratio analysis.

Ratio analysis is another method of calculation and analysis by which investment analysts often identify good-quality stocks. This method looks at a series of ratios that highlight profitability, liquidity, management effectiveness and a host of other characteristics. Each ratio has a general principle that indicates whether the company under scrutiny is better or worse than the average company in its sector. When that company is compared to other companies in the same sector, ratio analysis can help an investor arrive at a reasonable picture of a company's overall financial health and its outlook for the future.

Let's look at some of the major ratios for pairings of companies in the same industry. In all cases, the ratio results and the conclusions drawn by the Purple Chips method successfully identify the better of each pair of two companies.

Investment analysts consult many different ratios and financial yardsticks to assess the quality of an investment. Many of those instruments can demonstrate whether or not the company is better than average when compared to its peers. For simplicity, I will use three key ratios (see exhibit 2.17): five-year return on equity, five-year return on assets and five-year net profit margin. These three ratios are fairly broad in scope and therefore give an effective bird's-eye view of a company's health.

Exhibit 2.17 Financial Health Ratios

Ratio	General principle
5-year return on equity (net income / shareholders' equity)	Should be greater than 10%
5-year return on assets (net income + interest expense – interest tax savings) / average total assets	Should be greater than 10%
5-year net profit margin (average)	Should be higher than industry average

Exhibit 2.18   Con Edison (ED, May 2011)

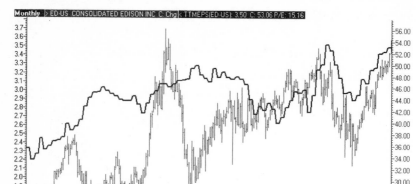

Con Edison versus Entergy

Our comparisons begin with two well-known U.S. utility companies: Con Edison (ED) and Entergy (ETR). They both provide power to the homes of millions of Americans. The graphs in exhibits 2.18 and 2.19 show both companies' respective EPS lines.

Exhibit 2.18 shows the volatility of Con Edison's EPS line. Since 1995, the EPS has hovered around $3 per share, plus or minus 50 cents. Note how the EPS has gone up and down with very little predictability; consequently, the stock price has been volatile.

In contrast, we see in exhibit 2.19 that Entergy's EPS line demonstrates a very steady upward progression and lower volatility. Exhibit 2.20 shows how the ratios of the two companies compare.

Using ratio analysis, one would conclude that Entergy has a better return on equity, return on assets and net profit margin than Con Edison.

With the Purple Chips approach, we can see that Entergy's EPS line shows a steady upward progression over the last twenty years, with much less volatility than Con Edison. The smoothness and predictability of Entergy's EPS line indicates that it is the superior investment when compared to Con Edison.

In conclusion, both methods of analysis have identified Entergy as being a better-quality investment.

Exhibit 2.19 Entergy (ETR, May 2011)

Exhibit 2.20 Con Edison and Entergy Ratio Comparison (data as of January 31, 2011)

Ratio	Con Edison	Entergy
Return on equity (ROE)	7.4%	13.7%
Return on assets (ROA)	2.3%	3.4%
Net profit margin	6.8%	10.1%

Source: MSN Money, http://investing.money.msn.com/investments/key-ratios?symbol=Ed&page=TenYearSummary, http://investing.money.msn.com/investments/key-ratios?symbol=ETR&page=TenYearSummary

Wendy's versus McDonald's

In the following example, we look at two well-known fast-food restaurant chains: Wendy's (WEN) and McDonald's (MCD). Having eaten at both, I would have trouble identifying the better company by the taste of their food alone. Once we examine their EPS lines, however, the choice becomes clear.

Wendy's operates about 6,500 restaurants, mostly in North America, which have the Wendy's or Arby's banner. McDonald's is a considerably larger global fast-food chain that has a presence in over one hundred countries.

The first clue about the quality of Wendy's stocks lies in the volatility of the company's earnings, as you can see in exhibit 2.21. In this case, the earnings are so volatile that they're off the chart!

Exhibit 2.21   Wendy's (WEN, May 2011)

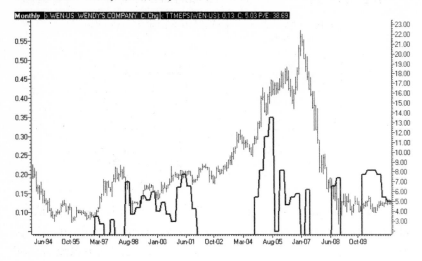

Exhibit 2.22   McDonald's (MCD, May 2011)

Second, you can see that over a ten-year period, Wendy's was not able to grow its EPS, which hovered at the break-even point, plus or minus $0.20 per share.

In exhibit 2.22 you can see that McDonald's EPS has grown steadily for the last seven years, from approximately $1.30 per share in 2003 to over $4.60 per share in 2011. Given the choice, which company would you rather invest in?

The ratios for the two restaurant chains follow:

Exhibit 2.23 Wendy's and McDonald's Ratio Comparison (data as of January 2011)

Ratio	Wendy's	McDonald's
Return on equity (ROE)	-6.7%	23.1%
Return on assets (ROA)	-2.6%	11.3%
Net profit margin	-6.8%	15.1%

Source: MSN Money, http://money.msn.com
http://investing.money.msn.com/investments/key-ratios?symbol=
wen&page=TenYearSummary, http://investing.money.msn.com/
investments/key-ratios?symbol=mcd&page=TenYearSummary

The ratio analysis in exhibit 2.23 indicates that McDonald's is clearly the superior restaurant chain to invest in. The Purple Chips approach also favors McDonald's because it has steady, predictable and growing EPS.

At this point, readers should be convinced that performance of earnings drives share prices. It is also clear that the EPS line is a valuable tool for identifying superior companies.

General Mills versus Kraft Foods

Next, we compare General Mills (GIS) and Kraft Foods (KFT). General Mills is a global food company best recognized for its popular consumer brands such as Cheerios, Betty Crocker and Green Giant. Kraft Foods is another global food titan, best known for Kraft Macaroni and Cheese (Kraft Dinner, in Canada) and other household brands, including Maxwell House and Oreo.

To the average consumer, Kraft is probably more familiar than General Mills, but the savvy investor will quickly see that General Mills is a better company to own.

Exhibit 2.24 shows the nice steady progression in General Mills' EPS. In the mid-1990s it was earning $0.70 per share; by the middle of 2010 it was earning over $2.30 per share.

Exhibit 2.25 demonstrates that perhaps Kraft is better at promoting its brands than at building value for its shareholders. Kraft's EPS has hovered around $2 per share since 2003, and consequently its stock price has languished.

Exhibit 2.24   General Mills (GIS, May 2011)

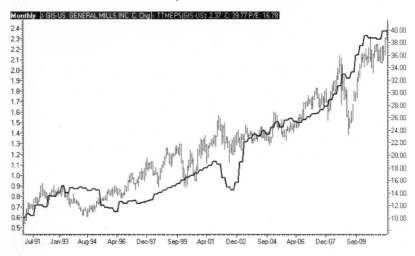

Exhibit 2.25   Kraft Foods (KFT, May 2011)

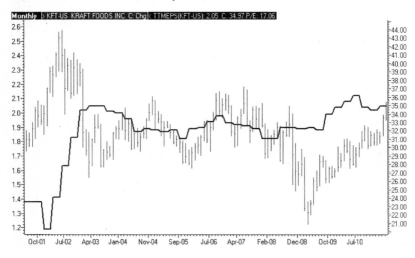

In exhibit 2.26 the ratio analysis leads to the same conclusion as the Purple Chips method. General Mills again rises above Kraft as the superior investment.

Simply put, companies are aware that investors look to sell their stock to another investor at a profit. So, to attract investors, companies have to grow their EPS.

Exhibit 2.26 General Mills and Kraft Ratio Comparison (data as of January 2011)

Ratio	General Mills	Kraft
Return on equity (ROE)	22.9%	9.7%
Return on assets (ROA)	7.0%	4.2%
Net profit margin	9.4%	7.2%

Source: MSN Money, http://money.msn.com
http://investing.money.msn.com/investments/
key-ratios?symbol=gis&page=TenYearSummary
http://investing.money.msn.com/investments/
key-ratios?symbol=kft&page=TenYearSummary

Google versus Yahoo!

In the following example, I compare two Internet titans: Google (GOOG) and Yahoo! (YHOO).

Yahoo! is best known as an early entrant in the Internet search arena; Google as the default search engine for most Americans and a leader in the sale of online advertising.

Exhibit 2.27 shows Yahoo!'s EPS as being stagnant from mid-2005 until March 2010.

Exhibit 2.27 Yahoo! (YHOO, May 2011)

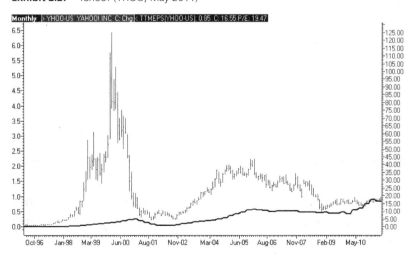

Exhibit 2.28 Google (GOOG, May 2011)

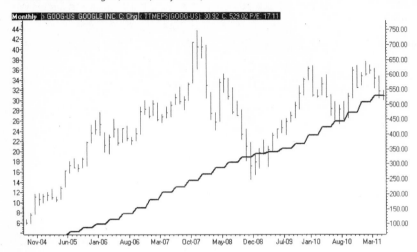

In exhibit 2.28 Google shows rapid and steady growth in earnings. Also noteworthy is the progression of EPS from about $4 per share in 2005 to more than $30 per share in 2011.

The ratio comparison in exhibit 2.29 shows that Google has posted a better financial performance than Yahoo!

We've seen in this chapter that the EPS line is a valid tool for comparing companies in similar sectors. The advantage of using the EPS line, however, lies in its comprehensive nature and easy identification. By looking for the hallmark of a steady and rising slope in the EPS line, an investor can identify a good-quality company that will likely experience an increase in its stock price as it grows its EPS.

Exhibit 2.29 Google and Yahoo! Ratio Comparison (data as of January 2011)

Ratio	Yahoo!	Google
Return on equity (ROE)	9.1%	17.1%
Return on assets (ROA)	7.3%	15.4%
Net profit margin	14.4%	25.0%

Source: MSN Money, http://money.msn.com
http://investing.money.msn.com/investments/key-ratios?symbol=yhoo&page=TenYearSummary,
http://investing.money.msn.com/investments/key-ratios?symbol=goog&page=TenYearSummary

CHAPTER 3

UNDERSTANDING AND
SEEING VALUATION

Now that we know what Purple Chips are and why they are so attractive to an investor, we have to know when to buy and sell them. While the simple rule of buy low and sell high applies just as much to our strategy as it does to any approach to investment, the method with which we find our entry and exit points is quite different. We saw in Chapter 2 that our approach to finding quality companies is simpler than traditional extensive ratio analysis in that we base our choices on the visual characteristics of an EPS line. Likewise, our way of deciding when to buy and sell is also simpler because it too relies on visual information. It is also very effective, and the reasons for its success will become clear in this chapter.

The Normal Curve: An Odds-Based Approach

The success of the Purple Chip model stems in part from its respect for what is known as the normal, or bell, curve. Exhibit 3.1 illustrates the

Exhibit 3.1 Normal Curve or Standard Deviation

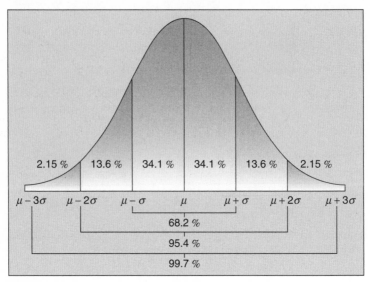

shape of the normal curve, which can be used to explain many things, including the behavior of share prices.

The theory behind the normal curve graph is that the peak in the curve, which is also called the mean or average, is where most activity occurs. The tail ends of the curve are any occurrences that are less likely to happen. In other words, they are further away from the norm, or are abnormal.

When applied to the stock market, the normal curve theory tells us that most of the time, or 68.2% of the time which the normal theory defines as one standard deviation on either side of the mean, stocks will trade around their fair value. Put another way, stocks will most often trade near their fair value or mean. Applying the normal theory to stocks indicates that stocks that trade at extreme high or low valuations are unusual. In other words, 95.4% of the time, stocks trade within two standard deviations from the mean, and 99.7% of all stocks trade within three standard deviations from the mean.

As I've mentioned, valuations usually fall closer to the high point of the curve than to its extremities. When a stock falls to the extremities of the curve, whether due to a high or low valuation, and there has been no change to the underlying fundamental situation of the company, the valuation of the company's stocks will most likely move back toward the center or high point of the curve. The Purple Chips model takes advantage of this knowledge by buying when the odds favor a return to the high point of the curve. We buy stocks when their prices are at a low valuation, and we sell them when the stock price has returned to normal, or positively exceeds the normal range, and becomes expensive.

The Purple Chips method has the greatest success when an investor applies its logic over a large number of potential investments.[1] By tracking dozens of Purple Chips stocks, an investor will be able to identify a few that are at attractive low valuations, while many will be at valuations that are normal.

The Shifting EPS Line: A Quick Gauge of Value

I mentioned in Chapter 2 that the graphs we use in the Purple Chips model are always set up so that the EPS line ends at the last trading price for the stock. This is deliberate. The two key lines in all the graphs, one for the EPS line and one for the stock price, are plotted on two different scales (the left and right y-axes). But the two lines could actually be placed anywhere on the graph relative to each other by simply changing the starting value of either of the scales. (Compare many of the charts in this book and you will notice that the y-axes do not always start at zero.) Ending the stock price and EPS lines at the same point on the chart provides the key to identifying a stock's current valuation. This layout allows us to determine not only the stock's typical market valuation (what the market considers to be its fair value in recent periods), but also its recent high and low valuations, and whether its current valuation is near the high or low.

Exhibit 3.2 is the graph for Johnson & Johnson (JNJ), a well-known maker of health care products and pharmaceuticals. It illustrates how well the EPS line gauges value, and will introduce the concept of the price/earnings multiple (P/E), which is simply the EPS multiplied by the stock price. On this chart there are four views of the same EPS line, numbered 1 through 4. The four views represent

Exhibit 3.2   Johnson & Johnson (JNJ, May 2011)

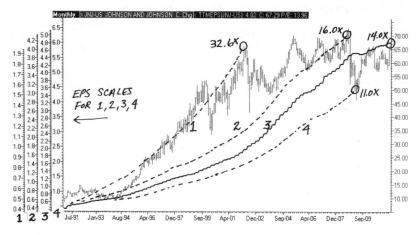

what the EPS line would have looked like when the stock was at the price where the EPS line ends. The corresponding scale for each EPS line is also numbered, and so EPS line number 1 should be read with scale number 1 on the left of the graph. Let me walk you through this graph. EPS line number 1 ends when JNJ was at $64.95 in March 2002 and the P/E was 32.6× (32.6× = 32.6 times—the × signifies times). EPS line number 2 ends when JNJ was at $70.43 in August 2008, and P/E was 16×. Note that the P/E is lower at this time than in 2002 even though the price is higher ($70.43 versus $64.95). EPS line number 3 ends when JNJ was at $67.29 in May 2011 and the P/E was 14×. EPS line number 4 ends when JNJ was at $50 in February 2009 and the P/E was 11×.

As we go from left to right the EPS lines become flatter, and the P/E multiple goes to 16× in August 2008, to 11× in February 2009 and to 14× in May of 2011. The key observation here is that the comparison of the slope of the EPS line at different times tells us how the stock is being valued. When the slope of the EPS line is steeper, it indicates that the valuation of the stock is higher and it is becoming more expensive. The opposite is true when the slope gets flatter; this means that the valuation of the shares is falling. You can see the falling valuation in

Exhibit 3.3 Johnson & Johnson (JNJ, May 2011)

exhibit 3.2, where the slope of the EPS line becomes flatter over time. Two key observations follow from this graph:

1. From 2002 to 2011 the market shifted toward paying less for every dollar of JNJ earnings.
2. The position of the EPS line relative to the range of prices at which the stocks were trading gives insight into the high and low valuation levels.

Exhibit 3.3 presents the same graph of JNJ, but here I prove that the different-looking EPS lines are all based on the same data. This is because the slope of the EPS line depends on where the stock price ended. In this example, we examine all of the EPS line values at March 2001. In each case, EPS lines number one through four all show a value of $1.74 at March 2001. The reason that the EPS lines look different is because the scales change as the EPS line follows the last sale price. In other words, if the last sale price of a stock goes lower, then the slope of the EPS line will flatten and the scale of that EPS line will be more compressed than when the EPS line is matched to a higher last sale price.

When we apply this concept—that the EPS line is the same for a stock but is moving with the last sale price—to the Purple Chips method, the EPS line becomes a valuable comparison tool for valuation. As can be seen on the graph in exhibit 3.3, a steeply sloped EPS line always indicates that the stock is at a higher valuation than it is at points where its slope is flatter. This concept is valid regardless of the stock price. Note how EPS line number two ends when JNJ was at $70.43 in August 2008 and the P/E was 16×. This valuation is lower than EPS line number one, which ends at $64.95. So in this case, even with a higher price, the valuation is lower. Why? It's because the EPS grew at a faster rate than the stock price. This trend becomes obvious by examining the slope of the EPS line. The illustration of this difference in the slopes of EPS lines is one of the key benefits of the Purple Chips approach. It demonstrates clearly where a stock is valued compared to its historical range of valuations.

Here's a question for the astute investor: Why use the EPS line when you could easily refer to a chart of the P/E ratio? Wouldn't this information be just as useful for determining interesting valuations? The answer is no. A chart of the P/E would not give as much insight into valuation.

Have a look at exhibit 3.4, which shows the chart of Wal-Mart with a graph of the P/E in the lower pane.

The P/E graph in the lower pane correctly shows that valuations are declining for Wal-Mart, but it does not offer enough insight to an investor who needs to know when to buy and sell. The P/E graph shows the steadily declining valuation of Wal-Mart since 2000, which is evidence of when the bear market began in many large value stocks.

In exhibit 3.5 we see that the same phenomenon of declining P/E values has affected Abbott Labs since early 1999.

The graph of the P/E ratio is interesting but offers little insight into when to buy and sell. Its usefulness to an investor is therefore limited.

At first glance, it may not be obvious that the trading range of the stocks that we are examining mirrors the shape of the EPS line. This notion becomes more evident, however, when one understands the concept of valuation resets.

Exhibit 3.4 Wal-Mart (WMT, May 2011)

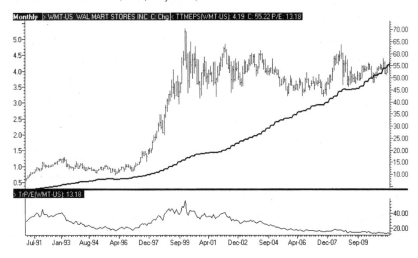

Exhibit 3.5 Abbott Labs (ABT, May 2011)

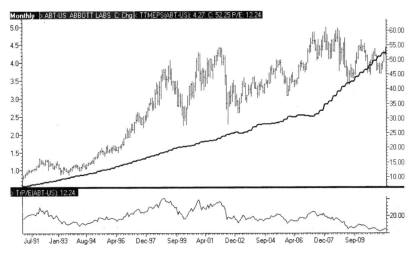

Valuation Reset

When you examine a company over a long period of time, you notice the phenomenon of valuation resets. This is the repricing of a security as the market decides to pay more, or less, for a company's earnings than it did previously. Valuation resets occur for many reasons, including shifting market sentiment, company-specific news that will affect future earnings or changes in regulations that have a direct impact on the earnings for an entire industry. Recognizing that a valuation reset has occurred is critical because it allows investors to realign their expectations to match those of the market.

The oceans' tides provide a simple analogy for how valuation resets occur when a change in sentiment is market-wide. When the tide comes in, everything floats to higher levels. This would be the case in what we call a "bull market," when all securities are increasingly priced at higher valuations. In bull markets, the valuation resets are all positive because investors will pay a higher P/E multiple for each dollar of EPS.

In the case of a receding tide, the trend moves in the opposite direction. In what we call a "bear market," everything drops to lower levels as investors now pay less for each dollar of earnings. The valuation resets that occur will be negative, which is typical for a bear market.

Whether it is produced by a bear market or a change that is specific to the company's operations, a negative valuation reset tells investors that they should expect the company's future valuation range to be lower. The market is telling investors that they can expect to pay less for each dollar of EPS.

Let's take a specific example. If a company was earning $1 per share and the shares were normally trading between a low and high valuation of 15× earnings and 20× earnings respectively, after a valuation reset the new valuation range could be 10× to 15× earnings.

Exhibit 3.6 shows a valuation reset of Abbott Labs. The dashed lines represent the EPS lines as they would have appeared prior to the valuation resets that are indicated by the arrows. These are significant because once a valuation reset has occurred, the trading range and valuation range of a stock shifts in the direction of the valuation reset. In the following example, you can see how Abbott Labs had been trading in a set valuation range for months or years, and then a valuation reset occurred (as indicated by the arrow) and Abbott Labs subsequently moved into a lower valuation range. The lower valuation range

Exhibit 3.6 Abbott Labs (ABT, May 2011)

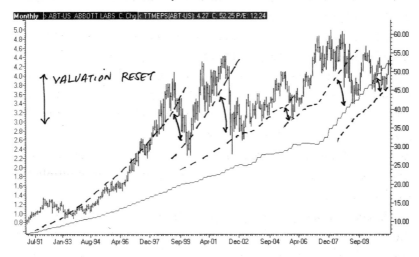

Exhibit 3.7 Abbott Labs (ABT, May 2011)

is evident because the stock price moved lower even though the EPS continued to move upward.

Exhibits 3.7 through 3.9 show valuation resets of Abbott Labs, Johnson & Johnson and Wal-Mart. In these charts we can see where specific valuation resets occurred. In exhibit 3.7 we see a series of positive valuation resets that started in 1991 and continued until 1999, followed by a series of negative valuation resets that were symptomatic of the developing bear market that followed. Note how the slope of the EPS line gets flatter after 1999. This indicates that the P/E multiples are increasingly lower in spite of the higher share prices. I mention this because one should never confuse a higher stock price with a higher valuation. The only way to know valuation is to be aware of the progression of earnings. For example, if earnings increase at a faster rate than the stock price, then valuation will decrease.

In exhibit 3.8 Johnson & Johnson displays similar characteristics: positive valuation resets until 1999, followed by negative valuation resets thereafter. Once again, note how the high P/E multiples decline after 1999 despite continued rising earnings per share.

Exhibit 3.9 demonstrates the valuation resets for Wal-Mart, with the shift in direction again happening after 1999.

It is difficult or impossible to know when a valuation reset will occur. The collective wisdom of the market dictates the new valuation range. Positive valuation resets are welcome to investors but negative ones are usually their bane. The best defense against a

Exhibit 3.8 Johnson & Johnson (JNJ, May 2011)

Exhibit 3.9 Wal-Mart (WMT, May 2011)

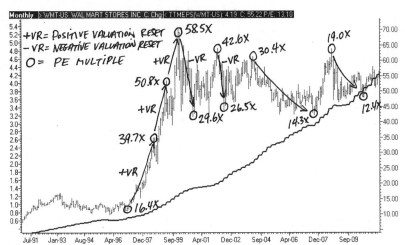

negative valuation reset is to purchase an investment when its valuation is low so that the market's repricing of the security, if it occurs, will be less severe. The best reaction to a valuation reset, whether the reset is positive or negative, is to adjust one's future expectations accordingly.

The Purple Chips model has a specific response to a negative valuation reset. When a stock has been purchased and a negative valuation reset occurs, the best strategy is to exit at breakeven at the first opportunity. This is because a valuation reset implies that the market has repriced a security so that the new range of valuations will be in the direction of the valuation reset. This will become more evident as we go through some case studies in Chapter 6. There we see that the buy and sell targets will be adjusted accordingly to the direction of the valuation resets. One of the advantages of the Purple Chips model is that even when a stock is purchased prior to a negative valuation reset, time works in your favor. This is because the basic premise of owning a Purple Chip is that the earnings will continue to grow, and this is exactly what works in your favor. As time passes, a Purple Chip keeps on making more money and this underpins the stock price. If the stock price has not increased, the growing earnings will make the stock attractive to investors, which will lead to a higher price. In the case of a positive valuation reset, these do not present any problem for an investor who has already bought stock. It means that his stock will be trading in a higher valuation range and she can expect to sell at a higher price than before the reset.

In conclusion, we see that the EPS line is an effective representation of a company's quality and that its slope can be used as a gauge of valuation. An EPS line with a flatter slope is synonymous with a lower valuation and a more steeply sloped EPS line indicates a higher or more expensive valuation. Lastly, when the EPS line is overlaid with the trading range of a stock, the EPS line can be used to determine the range in valuation.

CHAPTER 4

What Else You Need to Know

In this chapter, we discuss some of the background concepts that help support the foundation upon which Purple Chips is based. Do not be fooled by the title: this chapter is not an afterthought. The word "need" in the title was carefully chosen, as each of the topics covered here is essential to using the Purple Chips model successfully. These include earnings trends, valuation, the PEG ratio, building a portfolio of Purple Chips, value traps, limiting risk and more. After learning about these important elements that complete my presentation of the logic that supports this investment model, I show you how to buy and sell Purple Chips in Chapter 5, in Chapter 6 the model is applied in full to several case studies and then I offer my summary in Chapter 7.

Earnings Trend

Think singles and doubles versus home runs. If you recall from Chapter 1, the investment strategy that I propose is all about making constant profits rather than going for broke. We aim to hit singles and doubles, instead of going for home runs. As investors, our objective is to achieve a reasonable return with a low level of risk.

Once you understand that earnings are what determine the value of a company, you can take this logic one step further and realize that the progression of earnings influences the trading range of a stock. If a company shows that over the past year it has been growing its earnings per share (EPS) at an increasing rate, it is reasonable to expect that an investor will pay more for the stock because the future earnings stream is expected to be much larger. On the flip side, if the earnings are starting to decline, then an investor will pay less for the stock because the future earnings stream will be smaller. This effect can be seen in graphic form when the EPS line changes direction and the trading range follows. For an example, see the Lowes Companies (LOW) in exhibit 4.1. For many years Lowes enjoyed a growing EPS and then, in early 2007, its EPS began to decline and the trading range of the stock followed. By early 2010, the EPS resumed its upward trend and the trading range of the stock once again followed. This illustrates how earnings lead the trend in the stock price.

Now that we understand this relationship between earnings and the stock price, we show how to deal with a change in the trend of EPS after we've bought a Purple Chip.

Exhibit 4.1 Lowes Companies (LOW, May 2011)

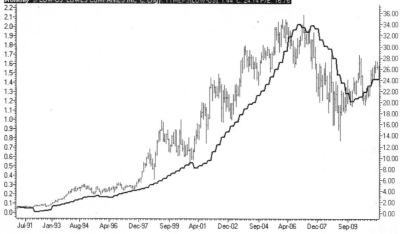

After making a purchase and determining the sell target for a stock (which you will soon learn), only imprudent investors would simply put it out of mind until it hits the selling price. Along the way, it is important to keep an eye on the company's earnings trend for validation that the plan is working. The trend in EPS is what determines whether we continue to hold a stock or sell it at a loss.

To ascertain a change in the earnings trend of a company, we look at the consistency of earnings and a change in direction. The evidence for this trend could be a single large drop in quarterly earnings or it could be a series of quarterly reports with no growth in earnings. These findings could be the precursor to a change in trend. Thus, the basic rule is that a change in the long-term EPS trend is significant if it is characterized by either of the following:

- earnings per share that have declined by an abnormal amount in one quarter; or
- earnings per share that have declined for three consecutive quarters.

When a change in trend is evident, the shares should be sold immediately, even if at a loss. Declining EPS is a red flag that indicates forthcoming problems. Remember that when a Purple Chip shows a change in its earnings trend, the new course is likely to continue for some time, just like an ocean liner changing direction.

Exhibit 4.2 shows that Home Depot behaved as a Purple Chip for many years before reporting its third successive quarter of declining earnings per share in June 2007, which indicated a significant change in EPS trend.

In exhibit 4.3 we see that by June 2008, Home Depot had reported successively lower EPS, and the share price quickly followed the declining EPS. Note that in the space of one year the share price went from $40 (when the change in EPS trend was evident) to less than $25.

Exhibit 4.4 shows how the EPS of Home Depot changed trend in 2006 and began to decline, and then began to trend higher in 2009.

Exhibit 4.2 Home Depot (HD, June 2007)

Exhibit 4.3 Home Depot (HD, June 2008)

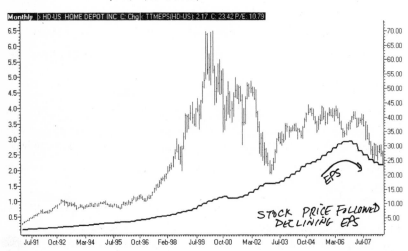

Note how the stock price fell to less than $20 in late 2008 as the EPS declined. Subsequently, the stock price recovered to more than $35 as the EPS began increasing. The rising EPS was a clear sign that Home Depot was recovering from its problems and that the stock price should begin trading in a higher range.

Exhibit 4.4 Home Depot (HD, August 2010)

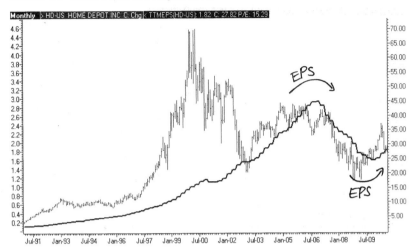

As can be seen from the preceding examples, stock prices often take months to adjust and properly reflect changes in earnings.

Value Traps

A value trap is something that should be avoided but is not easy to see; it is akin to catching a falling knife: It's an investment that appears to be attractive because it has a low valuation and a perceived low level of risk, but is, in fact, concealing a latent defect that has not yet come to the surface.

The Purple Chips approach seeks out investments that appear to be great value, but occasionally, it will lead you into a value trap. Value traps are often compared to catching a falling knife, because they can be dangerous to your financial health. To control the risk of being caught in a value trap, the Purple Chips approach defines risk at the outset.

In 2011, the best example of a value trap was Research in Motion (RIMM), which fell from approximately $60 per share to about $14 over the course of the year. Value traps tend to be more common when stocks are in a bear market because investors are less forgiving of disappointing events.

How does an investor protect himself from value traps? The answer is to limit risk by employing the two long-term EPS-based criteria that I described above. Purple Chips identifies opportunities based on the quality and trend of EPS, and it also uses the same metrics to limit risk.

The following example of Hudson City Bank (HCBK) shows how one bad quarter of EPS can dramatically change the long-term trend in EPS. In exhibit 4.5 we see that the last two quarters reported by HCBK were declining. Then on March 28, 2011, HCBK announced that its earnings had declined sharply in the latest quarter. At this time, the shares were still trading between $9 and $10, and the prudent investor would have sold his shares on this news.

One month later, in exhibit 4.6, HCBK is still hovering between $9 and $10, and the impact of the latest quarterly release is clearly visible as a break in the upward trend.

In exhibit 4.7 we can see that it often takes a few months for the impact of a significant change in earnings to be reflected in the price

Exhibit 4.5   Hudson City Bank (HCBK, March 2011)

Exhibit 4.6 Hudson City Bank (HCBK, April 2011)

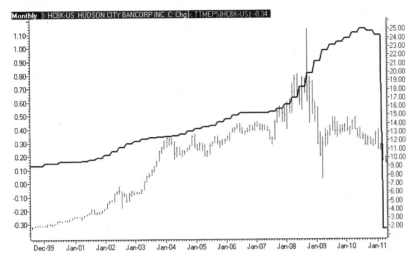

Exhibit 4.7 Hudson City Bank (HCBK, November 2011)

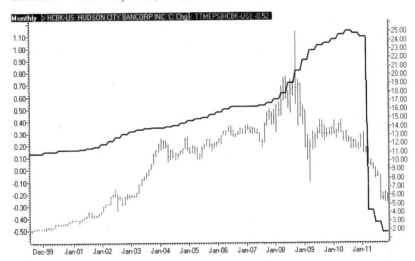

of a stock. By November 2011, the stock price of HCBK had fallen below $6.

Once a scenario occurs like the one above, where the earnings trend changes dramatically, the affected company is removed from the list of Purple Chips until it shows seven years of consistent, profitable growth in EPS. Purple Chips is based on trust and dependability, and such a company no longer satisfies these criteria.

Valuation Trend

Now we must understand valuation to be able to recognize buying and selling opportunities. Valuation can be expressed as a formula where:

$$\text{Valuation} = \text{Price/Earnings}$$
$$\text{Price} = \text{the stock (share) price}$$
$$\text{Earnings} = \text{EPS (earnings per share)}$$

For example, if a stock price is $30 and its EPS is $3, then the P/E, or valuation, is 10× (earnings). By the way, the terms "valuation," "P/E" and "P/E ratio" are often used interchangeably in the financial industry. To an investor, a lower valuation is always more attractive than a higher valuation because a low valuation is also considered less risky.

A simple analogy in the housing market can help to explain this concept. Suppose you hear of a house for sale in your neighborhood for $250,000 and you know that similar houses are selling for an average price of $300,000, and occasionally, for $350,000. In this case, the valuation range is $250,000 to $350,000. The $300,000 average price is what the market generally considers to be the fair price for such a house. At $250,000 we find the low end of the valuation range and at $350,000 the high end.

The valuation range will move up or down as the housing market changes. The average sale price may rise or fall if there is a change in supply or demand for such houses. Similarly, in the stock market, as information becomes available, a stock's valuation range will change. Information can take the form of company news, changes in the economy, a change in regulations that affect an industry and so on.

You can also think of valuation in terms of buying a business. If you pay $100,000 for a business that earns $10,000 per year, it will take you ten years to recoup your investment of $100,000. In this example:

$$\text{Valuation} = \$100{,}000/\$10{,}000$$
$$\text{Valuation} = 10\times$$
$$\text{Price} = \$100{,}000$$
$$\text{Earnings} = \$10{,}000$$

Suppose that you were able to buy the same business for $70,000. This would imply that you would recoup your investment in seven years (7× valuation), which is more appealing and less risky than waiting ten years to make back your money.

"Risk" is a relative term. To understand the level of risk that you are exposed to when buying a Purple Chip stock, you have to compare it to the valuation of the stock market. For example, we can use the widely-held S&P 500 Index as a proxy for the stock market. To find valuation, we take the Index value (price) and divide it by the sum of the earnings of each of the underlying companies that are its constituents. Therefore, if the S&P 500 is at 1,100 and the underlying companies are producing $68.75[1] of earnings per share, then the stock market P/E ratio would be 16×.

Generally, if a company valuation is lower than the market valuation, risk decreases. This is because there is a tendency for company valuations to revert to the mean, or market, valuation. We favor companies with low price/earnings (P/E) ratios because we want to construct a portfolio with many holdings and where the average P/E of the portfolio is lower than the current market P/E. For example, if the market P/E is 16×, then ideally our portfolio of investments should have an average P/E that is lower. How much lower is not easy to quantify, but as a rule of thumb, a portfolio that has an average P/E that is 5% lower or more is attractive. A portfolio with a low P/E is considered to be better and less risky.[2] There are exceptions to this rule, however. We will discuss this after we examine the reasons why low P/Es are attractive.

There are times when the P/E of the stock market makes it riskier to own stocks because the P/E of the market has a tendency to revert to more normal levels. Exhibit 4.8 shows you the P/E level of the S&P 500 Index from January 1, 1881, until November 17, 2011. When examining the chart, it becomes apparent that in the long run, the P/E ratio of the S&P 500 Index tends to average out around 15×. Secondly, one notices that the stock market can stay at or below average levels for years. In the words of John Maynard Keynes, the British economist, "the market can stay irrational longer than you can stay solvent."

Exhibit 4.8   S&P 500 Index P/E Ratios, 1881–2011

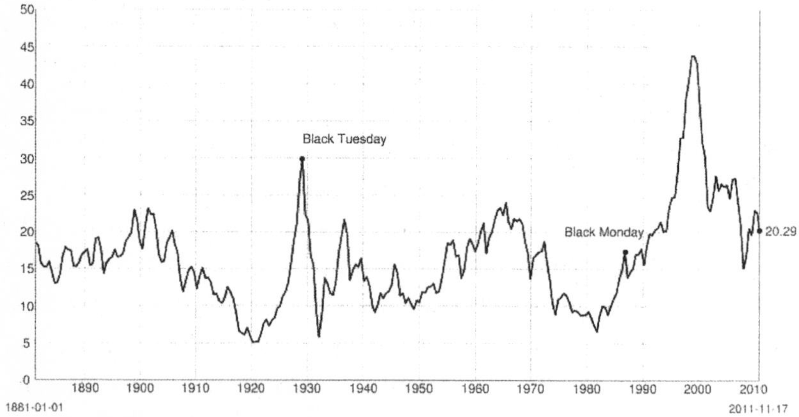

Data courtesy of Robert Shiller from *Irrational Exuberance*, Princeton University Press, 2000, 2005.

Professor Robert Shiller of Yale University is a well-known expert on the subject of P/E ratios and stock market returns. His research shows a strong connection between P/E levels and long-term returns. Based on his research, the conclusion was that ten-year returns are highest when the P/E ratios are lowest. Exhibit 4.9 shows the average ten-year rate of return for constituents of the S&P 500 Index from 1871 through 2012, based on their different P/E levels.

By definition, a bear market (jargon for a declining market) is characterized by declining valuations, or P/E multiples, and in a bull market (jargon for a rising market), valuations continue to rise as the bull market progresses. This trend occurs because investors will pay more for the same dollar of earnings, so P/E multiples rise. The opposite is true in a bear market. Investors will pay less for the same dollar of earnings.

Exhibit 4.9   S&P 500 Index: Expected Ten-Year Forward Real Returns

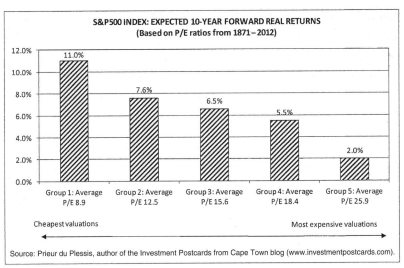

S&P500 INDEX: EXPECTED 10-YEAR FORWARD REAL RETURNS
(Based on P/E ratios from 1871–2012)

Source: Prieur du Plessis, author of the Investment Postcards from Cape Town blog (www.investmentpostcards.com).

The Purple Chips methodology is quite effective in revealing the market's long-term trend in valuations. By looking at changes in the range of P/E multiples for a few widely-held companies over an extended period of time, it becomes obvious whether valuations are generally rising or falling, and whether one should adjust expectations accordingly.

Valuation levels become obvious if you think of the slope of the EPS line as if it were the needle of a fuel gauge. In exhibit 4.10, when the gas needle goes lower (i.e., toward empty), it's time to fill up. Like the needle on the gas gauge, when the slope of the EPS line is lower (or flatter), you have to fill up (as in, buy more stock). The needle is like the EPS line and when it goes lower, it means the valuation has come down and the stock is more affordable.

In exhibit 4.11 the dashed line represents the EPS line as it would have looked when the stock price of Abbott Labs was at $61.09 in

Exhibit 4.10   Fuel Gauge

TIME TO FILL UP!

Exhibit 4.11 Seeing the Difference in Valuation—Abbott Labs (ABT, May 2011)

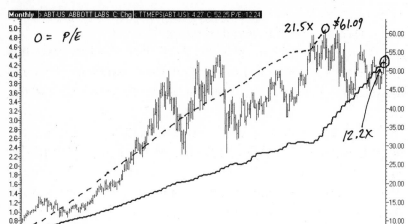

January 2008 and the P/E was at 21.5×. The solid black line is the EPS line when the stock price finished at $52.25 in May 2011. The slope of the EPS line is lower (or flatter) in May, which is consistent with a lower valuation and a lower P/E of 12.2×.

The following stocks provide good examples of how valuations change over time. Exhibit 4.12 shows that investors in Abbott Labs

Exhibit 4.12 Abbott Labs (ABT, May 2011)

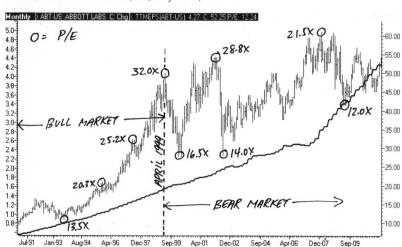

were paying around 15× earnings in the early 1990s and then, by April 1999, the valuation peaked when they were buying shares at 32× earnings (as seen by the vertical dashed line in the chart).

The opposite trend emerges after April 1999; the chart shows that investors began paying less for every dollar of earnings. This trend toward lower valuations has remained intact up to the time of this writing.[3]

In the early 1990s you see a typical bull market evolving with rising P/E multiples. After April 1999 the reverse is true. Bear market psychology takes over as the P/E multiple starts to compress in spite of Abbott Labs' rising earnings. Shortly after the peak P/E of 32× in April, the P/E drops to 16.5×, works its way down to 12.6× in May 2009 and then to 10.8× in January 2011.

Exhibit 4.13 presents the valuation of Johnson & Johnson over the same period of time, and we see a similar pattern to the one exhibit 4.12 revealed about Abbott Labs. The P/E peaks at 36× in November 1999, and then continues to decline progressively until it reaches its lowest point in March 2009, at 10×. This change coincides with a change in valuation psychology, which was seen in many large capitalization stocks during the same time period.

Exhibit 4.13 Johnson & Johnson (JNJ, August 2010)

Exhibit 4.14   Wal-Mart (WMT, August 2010)

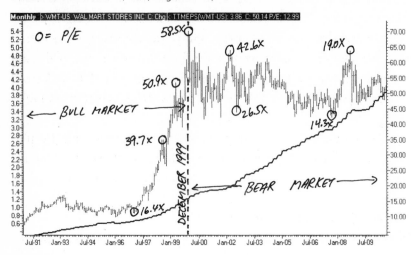

The same pattern is seen again in exhibit 4.14: Wal-Mart reaches a peak valuation of 58.5× in December 1999, and then begins a steady progression of lower valuations until August 2010.

Based on the preceding three examples, it becomes clear that these stocks have been in a bear market phase since late 1999 and have not given any evidence of a change in sentiment as of the time of this writing (August 2011). It also gives credence to a remark by John Mauldin, the popular market strategist, who said, "We should use valuations and not prices as the criterion for determining secular bull and bear cycles. If you use valuations, the cycles jump off the page at you. Using prices, it is very difficult."[4]

Being aware of the trend in valuation is advantageous to the patient investor because she can place her buy and sell targets at levels that are consistent with the direction of the trend. In the case of a bear market, where valuations are progressively lower, the investor will place her buy targets at a slightly lower level than the low end of valuations (as determined) and sell orders will be placed slightly lower than the high end of valuations. In the case of a bull market, the buy targets would be above the low end of valuations and the sell targets would be above the recent high end of valuations.

Valuations will also change over time as the company and all of the external factors that affect its value change. For example, if the company releases information that will positively affect future earnings, the EPS line, and consequently the valuation range, will rise. A positive change in a company's long-term outlook will be reflected in the EPS line as it rises more steeply, and a higher valuation and P/E multiple follow.

Now we must consider the growth rate in valuation. Some Purple Chips have high P/E ratios but this should not exclude every one of them for consideration in our realm of potential investments.

The P/E Ratio and Growth

The PEG ratio (also referred to as the PEG) is an abbreviation for "price/earnings growth." This ratio is used to look beyond the nominal P/E figure. The PEG ratio is a simple calculation that puts the valuation, or P/E ratio, in perspective. It looks beyond the nominal valuation figure and relates it to the rate of growth of a stock. It is calculated as follows:

$$\text{PEG ratio} = (\text{P/E})/\text{Growth rate}$$

For example, a company with a P/E of $10\times$ and a growth rate of 10% would have a PEG ratio of 1:

$$\text{PEG} = 1 = 10\times/10\%$$
$$\text{P/E} = 10\times$$
$$\text{Growth rate} = 10\%$$

Note that for this calculation, it is recommended that you use at least a three-year growth rate so that the result is more representative of average growth, and not simply the reflection of an exceptional year of growth.

The accepted principle to apply here is that if the PEG ratio is at 1 or less, then the company's stock is considered inexpensive or undervalued. For example, at the time of this writing, Google was trading at approximately $500 and it was earning approximately $33.21 per share, therefore the P/E ratio was $15\times$. Based on the information available at the time, Google was estimated to be growing earnings by 20% per year, therefore the PEG ratio was 0.75:

$$PEG = 15/20 = 0.75$$

If one believed that Google would continue to grow earnings at greater than 20%, then the PEG ratio tells you that Google is probably inexpensive at $500. The PEG ratio debunks the myth that a high P/E is always indicative of an expensive valuation.

Sometimes a stock will have all the hallmarks of a Purple Chip except that it will have a high P/E ratio, which we already know is synonymous with higher risk. The level of P/E is important because the stock market has historically traded around 15× earnings[5] and our preference is to buy Purple Chips that trade at a valuation that is not too far from historical norms. However, we do not want to exclude all companies from our model because of a higher-than-average P/E ratio. Tomorrow's leading Purple Chips would be excluded if we did not consider the PEG ratio. We would not look at great companies like Apple, Priceline or Google if not for the PEG.

The PEG ratio can also show that a low P/E may not be indicative of an undervalued company. For example, a utility that is growing at 4% and is trading at a valuation of 8× earnings would have a PEG of 2, which implies that it could be expensive. One must ask if the P/E level is realistic for the type of company being examined. This determination is subjective, and comes more easily with experience. For example, it would be expected that a utility company would trade at a lower P/E multiple than a fast-growing Internet-based business. A utility is a mature business that typically has slow growth and predictable revenues. By comparing a company's P/E ratio to its growth rate, we can better gauge the company's current valuation.

In addition, in a bull market, it may be difficult to find good companies that trade below the 15× average. Hence we have additional criteria, which incorporate the rate of growth. I discuss these in the buying and selling checklist in Chapter 5.

How to Build a Portfolio of Purple Chips

There are many books available that go into great depth on the topic of how to build a portfolio of investments. One simply has to search "portfolio management" on Amazon to find a lengthy list of books that cover the subject. In this section, I touch on the subject insofar as it concerns the implementation of the Purple Chips approach. My aim is to give some brief pointers so that you can minimize risk when assembling your portfolio. Every investor should be aware of his risk tolerance and understand that how he builds his portfolio is based on his own tolerance for risk.

Diversification

In the 1990s and earlier, it was common practice to diversify by investing in stock markets across the globe. It was believed that by investing in companies that were located in different countries, one could reduce the risk of a portfolio of investments because there was little relationship in the performance of stocks from different regions of the world. In essence, the theory was that when one stock market did poorly, another located elsewhere would probably be doing better.

Nowadays this theory is no longer valid. Diversification by investing in different countries is practically impossible. The correlation between markets in different countries is getting higher and higher as the world communicates more easily and businesses reach out across the globe to trade. Based on my experience, it is difficult to diversify by simply crossing borders, so I do not consider this to be a viable strategy for reducing risk when constructing a portfolio.

Diversification, however, is a valid concept when applied to different sectors. Sector refer to the area in which a company does business. For example, the resource sector has companies that are largely influenced by supply and demand for commodities. Examples would be companies in forestry, oil and gas or mining. The financial sector includes banks and insurance companies. The consumer discretionary sector includes retail stores such as Wal-Mart and Best Buy. Other sectors are health care, technology, industrial goods, services and utilities, among others.

Position Size

In addition to using the PEG ratio to evaluate risk, one can also control risk by adjusting the size of the investment in a stock. This is known as position size. Position size is the percentage weighting of a type of investment in a portfolio that a particular stock represents. It is commonly used to control risk and achieve diversification. Portfolio managers are taught that an average equity holding/investment in a portfolio should represent only around 5% of the total of equity holdings in the portfolio. This is because studies[6] have shown that an average portfolio only needs to have twenty different stocks (usually in different sectors) to achieve the maximum benefit from diversification.

When constructing a portfolio, I recommend that you never place more than 15% in one sector. In the securities industry, exposure to a sector is often referred to as being over- or underweight. Analysts will often say that they are overweight or underweight (which has nothing to do with the size of their body). This is jargon for being either over- or underexposed to a sector when their own weighting is compared to the index weighting.

The other factor that I consider when building a portfolio is how much capital to allocate to a particular stock. I use a rule of thumb of 5% for most investments. If a stock does not have a dividend and is considered riskier, I control risk by investing less. Stocks are usually categorized as value stocks or growth stocks. A value stock is defined as a large company that pays a dividend and is trading at a P/E multiple that is similar to, or lower than, that of the market. A growth stock is defined as a company that pays no dividend and has a higher than average rate of growth. My rule of thumb is 3% for non-dividend paying stocks (otherwise known as growth stocks).

Even though I do not recommend stop loss orders in Purple Chips, they do merit an explanation.

Stop Loss Orders

A stop loss order is an order to sell a security when it reaches a price that is lower than the current market price. It is designed to limit an investor's loss if a stock begins to fall. For example, if an investor buys Abbott Labs at $53 and places a stop loss order at $42.40, then he will sell Abbott Labs at the market price if the stock trades at or lower than $42.40. A stop loss order for the above would be entered (written) as:

SELL (QUANTITY) ABBOTT LABS @ $42.40 ON STOP

The hardest part about managing investments is knowing when to admit that you're wrong. A stop loss order takes the emotion out of this decision and forces you to take a loss when your pain threshold has been reached. I must emphasize that unless the stop loss order is actually placed in the market, it will do you no good. I can easily predict that a mental stop loss (i.e., a stop loss order that is not entered in the market but rather one in which an investor tells himself he will sell if a certain price is reached) is as good as useless. When the limit price of a stop loss is reached and the investor has not actually placed the stop in the market, the outcome is predictable. Here's what happens:

1. The stop loss price is reached.
2. The investor says to himself, "I'll just hold on to this stock a little longer because this is probably the lowest price."
3. The price goes lower. The investor says to himself, "Now it's really a bargain. I'll ignore the stop loss this time."
4. The price then goes much lower. The investor loses shirt and pants.

When I first developed the Purple Chips approach, I used stop loss orders to control risk, but I discovered over time that a rigid stop policy was hazardous to my financial health. There were a few occasions when I was stopped out of a Purple Chip at a loss, only to see it go back above my initial purchase price a few months later. Moral of the story: Like cream, quality always rises to the top.

Essentially, this is because stocks that fit the Purple Chips profile have a tendency to rebound and perform better than average, even in a market correction.

No More Anchoring

Another advantage of the Purple Chip method is that it avoids anchoring, one of the common pitfalls that investors fall into.

Anchoring occurs when an investor becomes attracted to certain price levels for buying or selling a stock because she believes that they represent reliable extremes that will recur. Unfortunately, this process is flawed because it ignores the relationship between price and EPS.

For example, an investor who anchors on a recent "high" stock price believes that a drop in price will provide an opportunity to buy the stock at a discount. While it is true that the fickle nature of the stock market can cause some stocks to drop substantially in price for no apparent reason, stocks quite often drop due to changes in their underlying fundamentals. There are two schools of thought in the financial industry regarding the price of stocks: that stock prices are determined by fundamental information or that prices are determined by technical information, also referred to as technical analysis.[7] "Fundamentals" is an industry term that is similar to a health chart for a patient in a hospital. In layperson's terms, fundamentals are all the factors that determine a company's financial stability and health. These can include, but are not limited to, earnings, sales, indebtedness, inventory levels and number of clients.

Exhibit 4.15 shows Whole Foods Market (WFM), a U.S.-based chain of supermarkets that specializes in natural and organic foods. Assume that in September 2004 an investor bought shares of WFM at $40 and subsequently sold them in June 2005 at $60 for a profit. Later in June 2007, the shares again traded at $40, so the investor buys again, thinking that he can repeat his previous experience. In essence, the investor believes that he has found an anchor point at $40, and presumes that the shares should again increase in value.

In exhibit 4.16 it becomes obvious that the investor who bought at $40 was right for only a very brief period of time. When the EPS

Exhibit 4.15   Whole Foods Market (WFM, June 2007)

Exhibit 4.16   Whole Foods Market (WFM, June 2008)

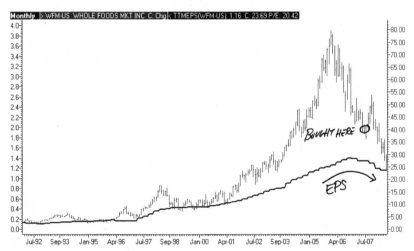

is overlaid on the chart it becomes clear that WFM stock was headed lower as earnings began to deteriorate. This proves that the price of a stock is driven by the direction of its earnings.

In theory, if there were no moving parts in the valuation of a company, dropping an anchor on a previously attained price might work well. However, because earnings and valuation levels change over time, anchoring can be a very risky practice. The Purple Chips model is dynamic because it establishes new buy and sell targets based on the latest developments in EPS, and on major high and low valuation points. Thus it protects investors from the pitfalls of anchoring.

Market Crashes

No discussion about losses would be complete without the mention of a stock market crash. We invest in Purple Chips only when their valuations are relatively low, which makes them inherently low-risk investments. But there will be times when we follow all of the guidelines suggested in this book and will still be caught in an unexpected market crash. A market crash is virtually impossible to predict. It is an event that is often talked about but rarely happens.

Market crashes are anomalies that can occur when stocks become overvalued, or events occur that are so severe that investors lose faith in the stock market. A market crash is a moment of irrational behavior, a repricing of all securities that is usually temporary. On September 9, 2001—(9/11)—there was a crash when America was attacked by terrorists and investors lost faith in the stock market. During a crash, all stocks are affected; there is no place to hide and the best defense is to invest in quality.

In conclusion, no plan is complete without well-defined entry and exit points. The rules for entry and exit points are absolutely essential to enforce discipline and maximize success. By becoming aware of valuation resets and trends in EPS, and by having a comprehensive investment plan, investors prepare themselves well for the surprises and challenges that the stock market inevitably poses for them.

Do It Yourself

There are websites that display separate earnings graphs and price charts, but the beauty of the Purple Chips approach lies in the simplicity of seeing the EPS line on the price chart and then determining valuation.

Securities industry professionals have access to Bloomberg and Thomson Reuters software that can easily replicate all of the charts used in this book, but for the do-it-yourself investor, the cost of these programs can be prohibitive. At the time of this writing, I was not aware of any free websites that overlaid the EPS lines on the price charts.

If neither you nor your money manager are able to access charts like the ones shown throughout this book, there are a few ways to replicate them. You can:

- Go to www.purplechips.com and access the latest Purple Chips stocks and supporting charts.
- Ask a securities industry professional to send you the charts of Purple Chips stocks you are interested in.
- Build your own charts.

Building your own Purple Chips charts requires only a few steps. Once the chart has been set up with the EPS line, it is easy to update the chart because quarterly results are added only four times per year. Follow these steps:

1. Print a bar chart for the stock in question.
2. Get your selected stock's trailing-twelve month EPS data going back a minimum of seven years. You can ask either an investment professional or the investor relations contact at the selected company for this information.
3. Determine the scale for the EPS by taking the lowest EPS figure less 30% and the highest EPS figure plus 30%.
4. Overlay the EPS data on the bar chart for the same time period.
5. Update the EPS line and price chart whenever the company issues a new quarterly result.

With practice, reading the EPS line as a measure for valuation, and picking out the high and low levels, becomes easier.

Now that you understand the relationship between EPS, stock price and valuation in Chapter 5, you will learn how to buy and sell according to the Purple Chips method.

CHAPTER 5

When to Buy and Sell

When you are ready to buy and sell Purple Chips, there are three steps to follow:

1. **On the chart, trace the shape of the EPS line at the high and low valuation levels.**
2. **Set the buy and sell targets.**
3. **As stock price or EPS changes, adjust the buy and sell targets.**

Step 1:
Draw the EPS Line

With practice, you will quickly learn how to gauge valuation by looking at the position of the EPS line. If the EPS line is in the low end of the valuation range for the last eighteen months of your time frame, then the odds suggest that the Purple Chip will return to the middle to high end sometime in the near future. Note that it is impossible to say exactly when this will occur, because it depends on the level of volatility of the stock market. If the stock market is in a period of high volatility, it is more likely that the time frame between high and low valuations will be shorter.

In exhibit 5.1 we can see that in September 2011 the stock price of Wal-Mart was at $51.90 and the valuation was at the low end of the range. The low valuation is evident because the EPS line is lower than the trading range of the stock. Recall that the EPS line always ends at the last trading price, therefore if Wal-Mart suddenly jumped to $65, the EPS line would have a much steeper slope and it would be obvious that the valuation had been lower when it was at $51.90 (as seen below).

Compare this to exhibit 5.2, just eight months earlier, in January 2011, when the stock price was $57 and the EPS line was clearly showing this Purple Chip to be at a higher valuation. Note how the slope of the EPS line is higher than most of the low trading prices between late 2008 and early 2011.

In exhibit 5.3 we can see that Abbott Labs was at a low valuation in January 2011. In fact, Abbott was actually at its lowest valuation in the last twenty years, as seen by the slope of the EPS line, which is the lowest or flattest that it's ever been.

Exhibit 5.1 Wal-Mart (WMT, September 2011)

Exhibit 5.2 Wal-Mart (WMT, January 2011)

Exhibit 5.3 Abbott Labs (ABT, January 2011)

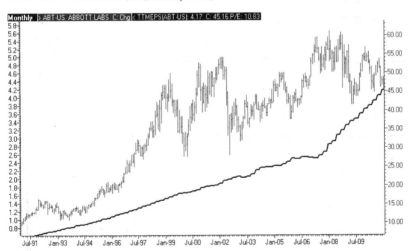

In exhibit 5.4 Abbott Labs was at a higher valuation just thirteen months earlier, in December 2009. Recall that valuations have trends (discussed in Chapter 4). This becomes obvious with Abbott Labs, as its valuation has been declining since early 2000. As a stock's P/E gets lower over time, an investor should be conscious that the trend could

Exhibit 5.4   Abbott Labs (ABT, December 2009)

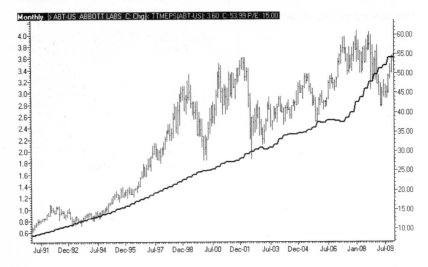

change at any time, which signals the beginning of a bull market, in which valuations will begin rising.

Step 2:
Set the Buy and Sell Targets

The valuation range is important because comparing the current stock price relative to its valuation range will tell you whether you should be buying or selling.

The upper part of this zone is where the stock is overvalued and the lower part of this zone is where it is undervalued, and where investors should look to buy. To determine a Purple Chip's valuation range, you extrapolate or project the earnings (EPS) line by following this step: Using the last eighteen months of data from the EPS line[1] (the last six quarters), trace the shape of the EPS line on the price chart so that it is bound by the stock price trading range and positioned at the highest level and the lowest level in the last eighteen months. The upper and lower valuation lines should end at the price scale, which indicates what you can expect for the range in stock price.

Exhibit 5.5 Becton Dickinson (BDX, October 2010)

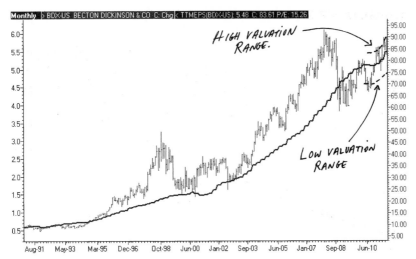

The valuation range is the area within the two traced lines. In exhibit 5.5, using Becton Dickinson (BDX), we trace the shape of the EPS line for the last eighteen months and identify the high and low valuation range. Based on this, the valuation range is between $75 and $90.

Note that because the EPS lines are evolving with the passage of time, the valuation range will follow the shape of the EPS line. If the EPS line flattens, then the valuation range will flatten as well. If the EPS continues its growing trend (as should be the case with most Purple Chips—recall the ocean liner analogy), then it would be expected that the trading range would shift higher with the growing EPS. The valuation range is dynamic because it is a function of the developing earnings.

Step 3:
Adjust the Buy and Sell Targets

Step 2 showed us where the high and low end of the valuation range was. Now, we can take this range and substitute it for our buy and sell targets.

Before setting buy and sell targets for a stock, one must be aware of the trend in valuation. By knowing where valuations are going, an investor can make money, even if valuations are falling. This is because bull and bear markets are characterized by a lot of zigging and zagging. Trends rarely follow a straight line because valuations rise and fall. For example, in a bear market high valuations are progressively lower and low valuations are progressively lower. The opposite is true in a bull market.

One last point: When targets are set, I specifically avoid using round numbers, as this tends to be where orders accumulate and decreases your chances of execution. Buy targets are always just above the round figure and sell targets are always just below the round figure.

Once a Purple Chip is in the buying or selling zone, an investor should go through the appropriate checklist prior to acting:

Buying Checklist

1. If the P/E is greater than 15×, the PEG ratio should be less than 1.
2. If the P/E is less than 15×, the PEG ratio should be less than 1.3.
3. Verify news sources for any impending threats that could alter the trend in EPS.
4. Is it a bull or a bear market? Will the current trend in valuations lead to lower or higher valuations?
5. Avoid the use of round numbers. A buy order should always be placed above the round figure (e.g., Place buy at $20.10 instead of $20).

Selling Checklist

1. Is the stock likely to remain expensive for a few more quarters?
2. Are there any impending developments that will cause EPS to accelerate in the coming months and lead to even higher prices and valuations?
3. What is the current trend in valuations? Is it a bull or a bear market?
4. Avoid the use of round numbers. A sell order should be placed below the round figure (e.g., Place sell at $19.90 instead of $20).

With regard to the first item on the selling checklist, Church & Dwight (CHD) is a good example of a stock that remained expensive

Exhibit 5.6 Church & Dwight (CHD, February 2011)

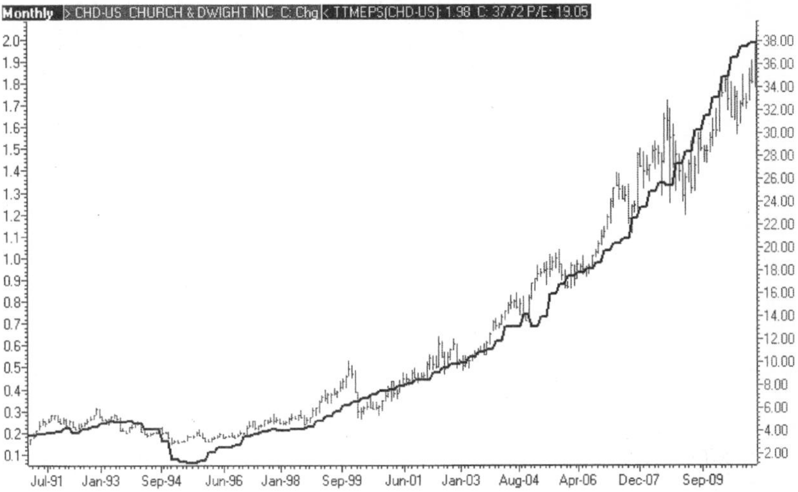

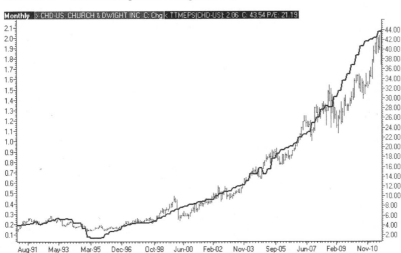

for several quarters after reaching the high end of valuations. Exhibit 5.6 shows that CHD was in the selling zone in February 2011.

In exhibit 5.7, six months later, in August 2011, CHD was still expensive, yet the price was almost $6 per share higher. Note that the Purple Chips approach doesn't attempt to squeeze out every penny of

Exhibit 5.7 Church & Dwight (CHD, August 2011)

Exhibit 5.8 Apple (AAPL, June 2011)

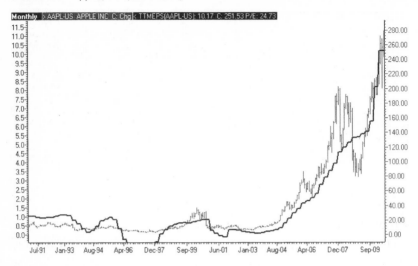

potential profit. The objective is to consistently make profits and move on to the next opportunity once a stock has reached a high valuation.

Apple is a good example of a stock with accelerating earnings. In exhibit 5.8 we see that EPS accelerated starting in early 2010. Before that, Apple had consistent growth in EPS and then it began to skyrocket. This coincided with huge gains in market share for Apple because of the success of its iPhone. Naturally, the stock price followed the rising EPS. As was mentioned in the selling checklist, when a Purple Chip stock's EPS begins accelerating, there is a high likelihood that prices will continue rising and therefore one should not rush to sell.

In the next example we see what happens in a bull market when valuations keep on rising. For this, we go back to 1993 and look at Procter & Gamble (PG). Exhibit 5.9 shows how the S&P 500 Index evolved between 1993 and 1999. Note how the valuation of the Index passed from 13.8× earnings in 1994 to 30.7× earnings in 1999.

Knowing that the stock market was in a bullish trend and that valuations were rising would influence how you would position your buy and sell targets. In a bull market, you could expect valuations to rise over time; therefore you would want to place your buy orders slightly higher than the low valuation range that was identified by the Purple

Exhibit 5.9   S&P 500 Index, P/E Ranges 1993–1999

Year	Low	High	Earnings	Low valuation (P/E)	High valuation (P/E)
1999	1205.46	1473.13	51.02	25.39	30.72
1998	912.83	1244.93	44.33	20.26	28.08
1997	729.55	986.25	45.06	17.33	22.30
1996	597.29	762.12	41.05	15.45	19.14
1995	457.20	622.88	37.77	14.26	16.53
1994	435.86	482.85	32.07	13.81	17.62
1993	426.88	471.29	27.41	15.57	17.19

Chips approach. In the following example of Procter & Gamble, you will see that you would miss some good entry points if you ignored the influence of a bull market. In addition, you can also adjust selling targets above the high valuation level to account for valuations that are rising. For simplicity, I present graphs that were updated every six months with buy and sell targets. Note that in practice, you must have the buy and sell targets defined at all times and be ready to update them as soon as a new earnings figure is released (every quarter). In exhibit 5.10 the buy and sell targets are identified as $11.75 and $15.

Exhibit 5.10   Procter & Gamble (PG, March 1993)

Exhibit 5.11 Procter & Gamble (PG, September 1993)

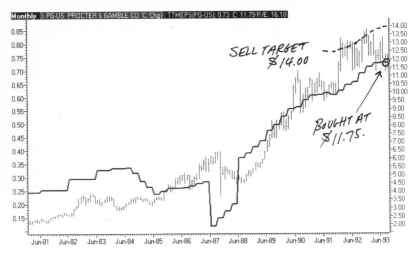

In exhibit 5.11, in the next six months, the stock had dropped to $11.23, so a buy order was executed at $11.75 and a sell order would have been placed at $14 based on the profile of the EPS line.

In exhibit 5.12, by March 1994 the stock had risen and the sell order was executed at $14. The new buy target was set at $12.50 based on the shape of the EPS line.

Exhibit 5.12 Procter & Gamble (PG, March 1994)

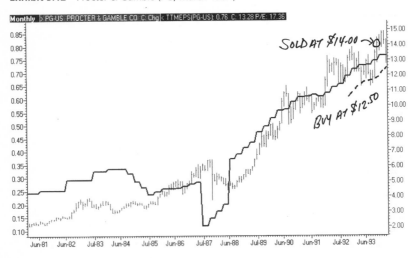

Exhibit 5.13 Procter & Gamble (PG, September 1994)

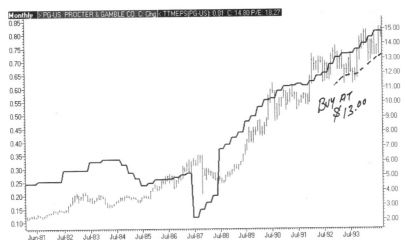

In exhibit 5.13 the buy target was adjusted upward to account for the increase in EPS.

In exhibit 5.14 we see that PG shares continued to rise as the EPS increased and the buy target was raised to $15.50.

In exhibit 5.15 the stock had risen to $19 and we were not able to buy it because there were no significant corrections in price that

Exhibit 5.14 Procter & Gamble (PG, March 1995)

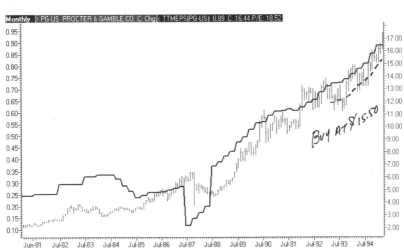

Exhibit 5.15 Procter & Gamble (PG, September 1995)

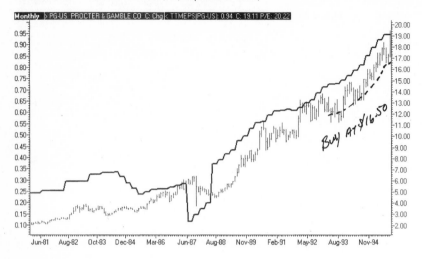

made the valuation attractive. Due to the rising EPS, the buy target was raised to $16.50.

The preceding example shows that the Purple Chips model was effective in pointing out value, but it also illustrates the challenge posed by a bull market. Investors have to be patient because corrections are small and prices keep on rising. My advice is the following: If you miss one opportunity, look elsewhere because there will be others.

In the next chapter, we apply all of our knowledge of Purple Chips to four case studies that highlight the many scenarios that can occur while investing in the stock market.

CHAPTER 6

PRACTICE CASE STUDIES

In the following case studies, I demonstrate how the Purple Chips method would have acted on four Purple Chips: Abbott Labs, AutoZone, Johnson & Johnson and General Dynamics. Each of these was chosen to highlight the multitude of scenarios that can unfold after one has invested. In addition, the examples begin in late 1999 when the bear market in valuations was just beginning. This reinforces the notion that valuations tend to behave in a gradual fashion of zigging and zagging over time, and that in spite of a general pattern of declining valuations in the stock market, investors can still profit if they invest at the right valuation. As we've learned throughout *Purple Chips,* company valuations rarely change dramatically unless there is company-specific news that changes the future earnings stream. Fortunately, Purple Chips are predictable stocks that have a history of avoiding surprises, much like the ocean liner that charts its course through the sea.

During the crash of 2008 and 2009, many of the transactions in the examples resulted in break-even trades because there were valuation resets after the purchases were initiated. Recall that in such a case, the Purple Chips methodology states that you should sell once the stock price is at breakeven and then attempt to buy at the newly established low end of the valuation range. In spite of these fruitless transactions, the Purple Chips method did result in reasonable profits over the investment time periods.

These examples show the validity of a long-term valuation-based approach. The purpose is not to show that there was an exact point where a Purple Chip should have been bought or sold. Rather, it is to show that by applying the Purple Chips method, we are able to identify low and high valuation points that are likely to have a high probability of being outside the normal valuation. One last point: recall what was mentioned in Chapter 5, that when targets are set, avoid using round numbers. Buy targets are always just above the round figure and sell targets are always just below the round figure.

Each case study begins with a visual recap that shows a chart with buy and sell points over the period examined. Then, on a regular basis, we examine the charts the way they looked at particular points in time and highlight any adjustments that were made in the strategy. We conclude the case studies by showing a recap of the transactions in tabular form along with an estimate of the percentage of time that an investor would have been invested over the time period examined. The amount of time invested is important because I emphasize that the Purple Chips way of investing is more interesting than the traditional buy and hold strategy because you do not tie up your capital for an extended period of time. The advantage of Purple Chips is that when you exit a position, you can recycle your capital into another low-risk opportunity.

Case Study: Abbott Labs

Abbott Laboratories (ABT)—a major pharmaceutical company engaged in the discovery, development, manufacture and sale of a diversified line of health care products—is one of the top Purple Chips.

In exhibit 6.1 we see the different valuations of ABT over a twenty-year period and note that the declining slopes of the EPS lines indicate that valuations were dropping since 1999. The dashed EPS lines show what the EPS line looked like when it was at the price where the EPS line ends. The EPS scale on the left side of the graph is only for the April 2009 EPS line.

Exhibit 6.2 shows the EPS at each point in time and the corresponding valuation, or P/E level. Again, we notice how the EPS line is

Exhibit 6.1 Abbott Labs (ABT, April 2009)

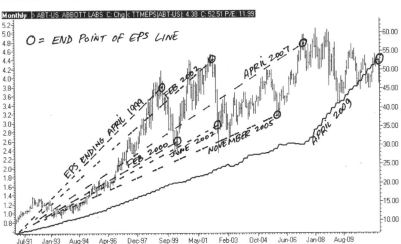

Exhibit 6.2 Abbott Labs Valuation Range

Date	Stock price	EPS	P/E (Valuation)
Apr. 1999	$45.25	$1.56	29×
Feb. 2000	$30.87	$1.66	18.6×
Feb. 2002	$52.89	$1.88	28.1×
June 2002	$35.22	$1.99	17.7×
Nov. 2005	$37.71	$2.41	15.6×
Apr. 2007	$56.62	$2.50	22.6×
Apr. 2009	$41.85	$3.42	12.2×

Exhibit 6.3 Abbott Labs (ABT, August 2011)

a valid gauge of valuation as its slope gets steeper with high valuations and flatter with lower valuations. The slope of the EPS line illustrates that, in April of 1999, Abbott had its highest valuation at 29× earnings and its lowest valuation in April of 2009 at 12.2× earnings.

In exhibit 6.3 we see how Purple Chips would have bought and sold Abbott Labs between April of 1999 and August of 2011. Note that two break-even transactions are visible on the chart, one where Abbott was bought and sold in the space of a month, and the other where Abbott was bought and then sold at breakeven only thirteen months later.

In exhibit 6.4 we begin in April 1999 by projecting the EPS line from a low valuation point that was established in 1996. Note that in April 1999, Abbott has a very high P/E ratio of 29×, therefore caution is necessary. In some cases, the Purple Chips approach will not invest because valuations, and therefore risk, are simply too high.

By December of 1999 (see exhibit 6.5), Abbott has a correction and we buy the stock for the first time at $33.10. Note that the P/E at this time is more reasonable at 20.7× earnings. Based on the shape of the EPS line, we project that Abbott will be at a high valuation at $46.90, which corresponds to our selling target.

Exhibit 6.4   Abbott Labs (ABT, April 1999)

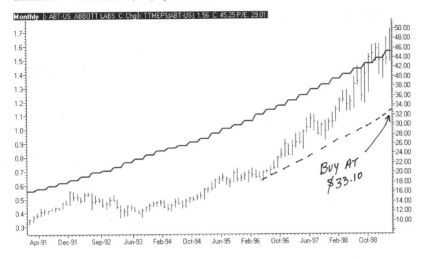

Exhibit 6.5   Abbott Labs (ABT, December 1999)

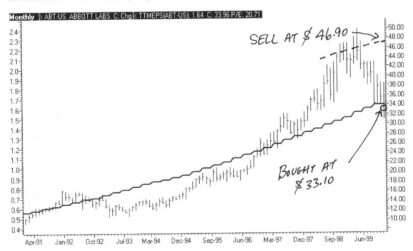

Exhibit 6.6 shows that Abbott starts to climb, and based on the shape of the EPS line, the sell target is still at $46.90.

In exhibit 6.7 Abbott reaches the sell target and we sell at $46.90 in October 2000. Based on the shape of the EPS line at the time, we now conclude that the low end of valuations will be $35.10.

Exhibit 6.6   Abbott Labs (ABT, May 2000)

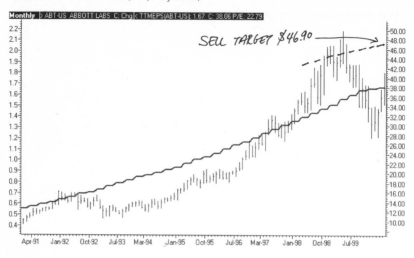

Exhibit 6.7   Abbott Labs (ABT, December 2000)

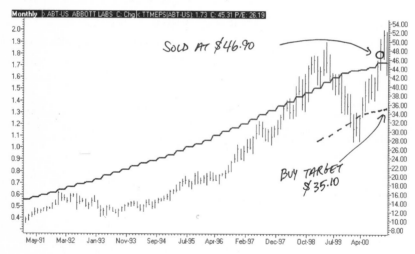

In exhibit 6.8 Abbott continues to rise in price and the EPS continues to rise with each quarter. Based on this, we adjust our buy target to $37.10 and wait for a low valuation to re-enter. Note how the high valuation is clearly visible at this point as the EPS line is in the high end of its historical range.

Exhibit 6.8 Abbott Labs (ABT, December 2001)

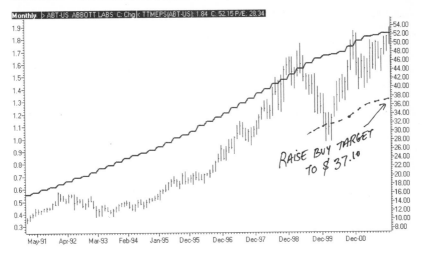

Exhibit 6.9 shows that we buy Abbott in July of 2002 at $37.10 based on the shape of the rising EPS line. Unfortunately, in the following month Abbott experiences a valuation reset when it trades as low as $27.87. As was mentioned in Chapter 3, when such an event occurs, it is best to sell at breakeven and attempt to buy again only at the newly established low end of the valuation range.

Exhibit 6.9 Abbott Labs (ABT, July 2002)

Exhibit 6.10 Abbott Labs (ABT, August 2002)

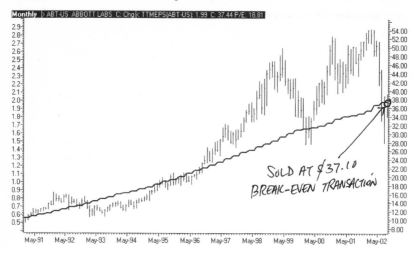

Exhibit 6.10 shows that Abbott bounces upward following its valuation reset and allows us to sell at breakeven. Now we can re-examine the range of valuations and establish a new buy target.

In exhibit 6.11 we establish that the low end of the valuation range is at $34.10 and we buy at this level. We also set our sell target by

Exhibit 6.11 Abbott Labs (ABT, February 2003)

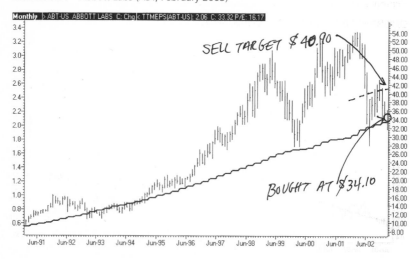

Exhibit 6.12   Abbott Labs (ABT, June 2003)

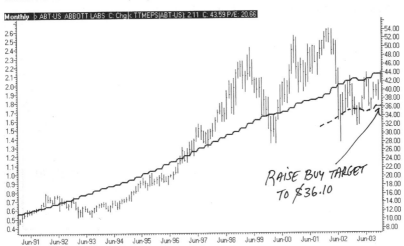

projecting the EPS line off the high end of the recent stock price trading range at $40.90.

In exhibit 6.12 we reach our sell target in May and sell Abbott at $40.90. We then establish our new buy target at $34.10.

In exhibit 6.13, based on the improvement in EPS, we raise our buy target to $36.10. Note that Abbott has one quarter of declining EPS (two quarters back). This is one of the principal reasons why

Exhibit 6.13   Abbott Labs (ABT, December 2003)

Exhibit 6.14   Abbott Labs (ABT, June 2004)

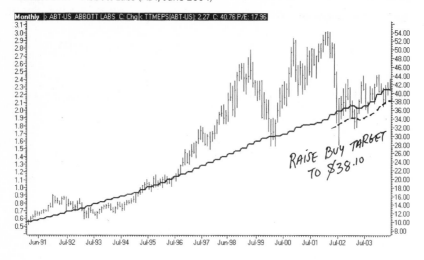

Purple Chips are attractive: They seldom deviate from their trend of growing EPS.

In exhibit 6.14 we raise the buy target to $38.10 because the EPS has risen.

In exhibit 6.15 we raise our buy target to $39.10 because the EPS is rising.

Exhibit 6.15   Abbott Labs (ABT, December 2004)

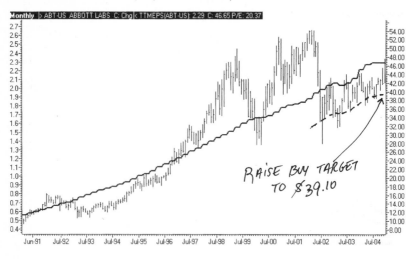

Exhibit 6.16 Abbott Labs (ABT, June 2005)

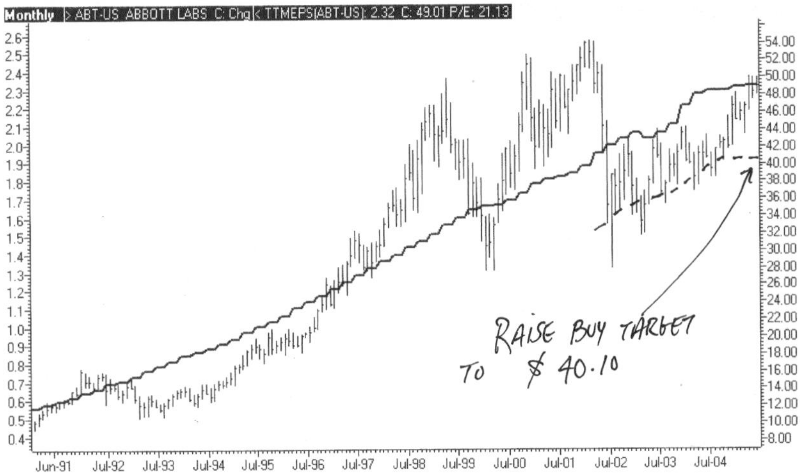

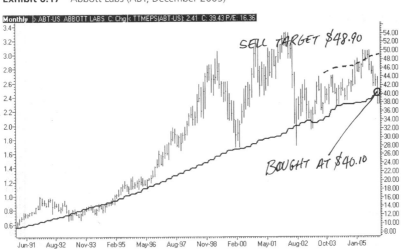

In exhibit 6.16 we raise the buy target to $40.10 as the EPS contin-
ues to rise. Investing in Purple Chips requires an enormous amount
of patience and discipline because sometimes you may be forced to sit
on the sidelines for years as a stock appreciates and remains at a high
valuation.

In exhibit 6.17 we see that our patience is rewarded, and we buy
at $40.10 in November of 2005. Based on the shape of the EPS line,

Exhibit 6.17 Abbott Labs (ABT, December 2005)

Exhibit 6.18   Abbott Labs (ABT, June 2006)

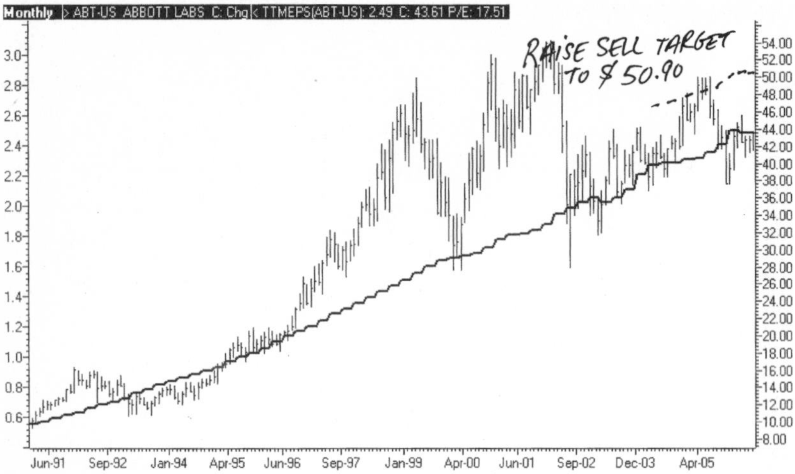

we see the high end of the valuation range and set the sell target at $48.90.

In exhibit 6.18 we raise the sell target to $50.90 because the EPS continues to improve (this is not surprising for a Purple Chip).

In exhibit 6.19 we adjust our sell price upward to $51.90 on rising EPS and manage to sell at $51.90 in January. We then estimate that the

Exhibit 6.19   Abbott Labs (ABT, January 2007)

Exhibit 6.20 Abbott Labs (ABT, December 2007)

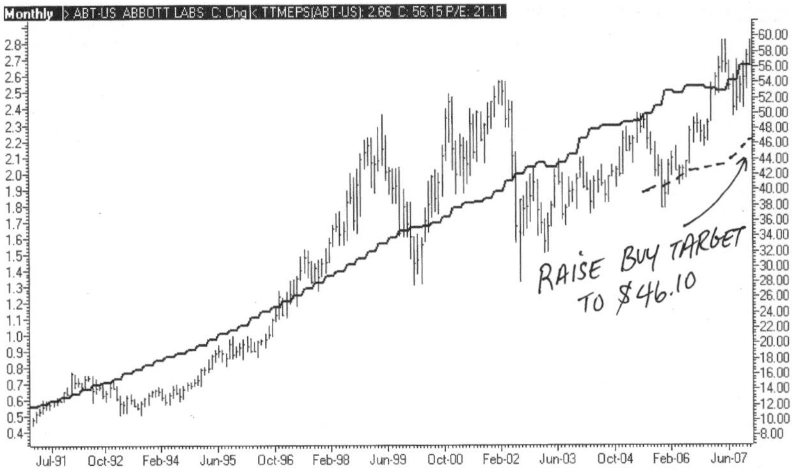

low end of the valuation range will be around $42, so we place our buy target at $42.10.

In exhibit 6.20 we raise our buy target to $46.10 because of the rising EPS.

In exhibit 6.21 we adjust our buy target upward to $47.10 as the EPS continues climbing.

Exhibit 6.21 Abbott Labs (ABT, June 2008)

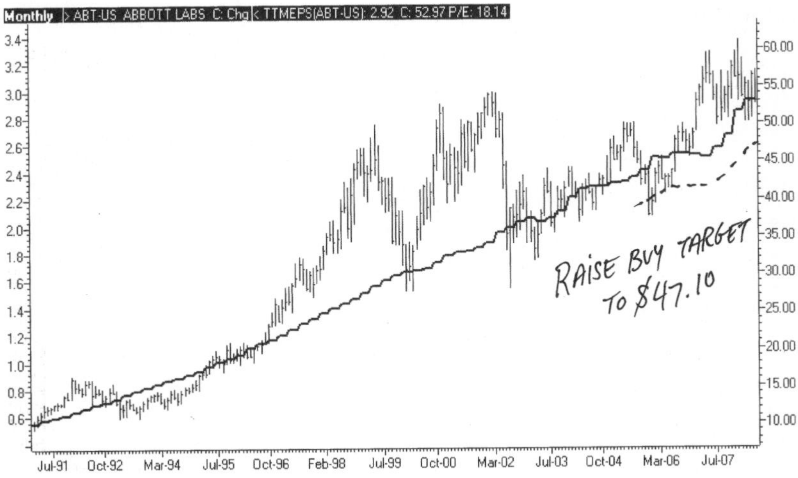

Exhibit 6.22 Abbott Labs (ABT, December 2008)

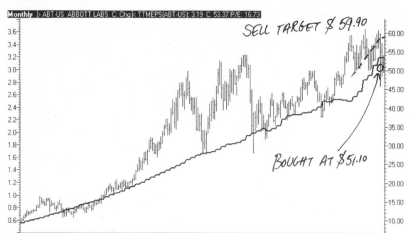

In exhibit 6.22 we adjust our buy target upward because of rising EPS and manage to buy at $51.10. We simultaneously establish the sell target at $59.90. Note that Abbott is now trading at a much more reasonable P/E of 16.7×. Recall that in late 1999, when we began this case study, Abbott was trading around 29× earnings. The valuation decreased over time because the earnings grew faster than the stock price. This demonstrates why Purple Chips are of a better quality than the majority of stocks: Purple Chips consistently grow their earnings, which consequently underpins the stock price.

In exhibit 6.23 we see that Abbott experiences a valuation reset when the stock price trades as low as $41.27. Based on this, we know we must sell at $51.10 (the price at which we most recently bought the stock), in order to break even, and then try to buy at the low end of the new valuation range. This period coincides with the climax of the credit crisis and, in retrospect, not surprisingly this was the time when most stocks reached their lowest prices, when fear and uncertainty dominated investor sentiment.

In exhibit 6.24 we manage to sell at $51.10 after waiting patiently for nearly six months. Now the buy target is set at $46.10 based on the low end of the valuation range.

Exhibit 6.23 Abbott Labs (ABT, June 2009)

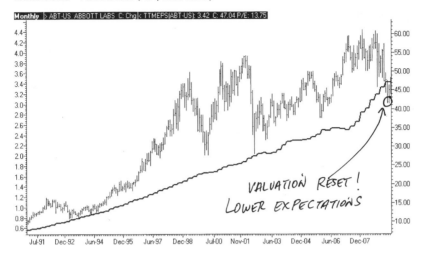

Exhibit 6.24 Abbott Labs (ABT, December 2009)

In exhibit 6.25 we succeed in buying at $46.10 in May of 2010. The sell target is set at $54.90 based on the shape of the EPS line at the time.

In exhibit 6.26 we move the selling target upward to $55.90 because the EPS has risen.

In exhibit 6.27 it is seven months later and our sell target remains at $55.90.

Exhibit 6.25 Abbott Labs (ABT, June 2010)

Exhibit 6.26 Abbott Labs (ABT, December 2010)

Exhibit 6.28 shows that the Purple Chips approach had the following results with Abbott Labs:

Abbott Labs Case Study Summary

- The stock price of Abbott Labs was fairly volatile over the years and consequently presented some very good opportunities for followers of Purple Chips. In spite of the stock price volatility, the upward

Exhibit 6.27   Abbott Labs (ABT, August 2011)

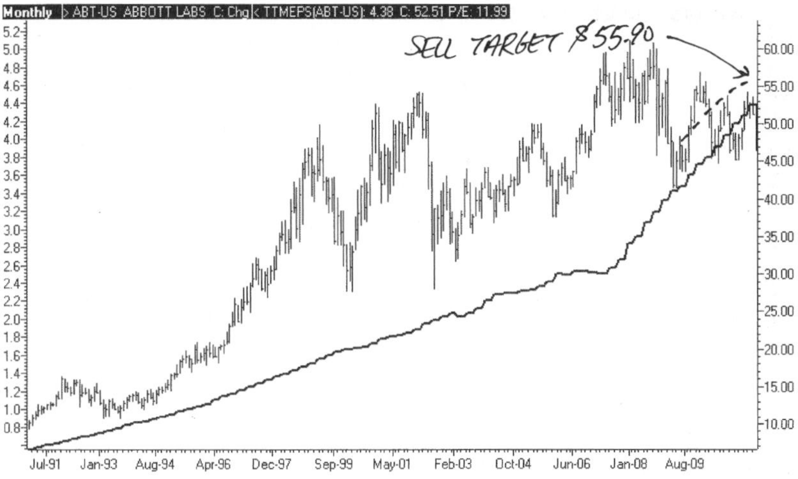

Exhibit 6.28   Purple Chips Results for Abbott Labs*

Abbott Labs				
Date	Buy	Date	Sell	Gain/Loss
Dec. 1999	$33.10	Oct. 2000	$46.90	$13.80
June 2002	$37.10	July 2002	$37.10	$ 0.00
Feb. 2003	$34.10	May 2003	$40.90	$ 6.80
Nov. 2005	$40.10	Jan. 2007	$51.90	$11.80
Oct. 2008	$51.10	Oct. 2009	$51.10	0.00
June 2010	$46.10	?**	?**	?**
			Total gain/loss	$32.40

*% of time period invested in stock (as of Aug. 2011): 61 months/141 = 43%.

**This investment had not been closed, so the outcome was unknown.

progression in earnings continued with very few aberrations. Based on the case study of Abbott Labs, we believe that the Purple Chip method demonstrates its worth as a low risk/high performance approach to investing. Between the years 1999 and 2011 the price of Abbott shares ranged from $27.48 to $61.09, yet the Purple Chips method captured $32.40 per share in profit.

- The investor who followed the Purple Chips approach was invested in this stock for 61 months out of the 141 months in this study or for only 43% of the time period that was covered.

Case Study: AutoZone

This example illustrates how Purple Chips would have fared on a company that experienced stellar growth in earnings. AutoZone is considered a growth stock because it pays no dividend and trades at a higher multiple than many Purple Chips. As mentioned in Chapter 4, when we invest in growth stocks, we recommend taking a smaller position size (around 3%) to mitigate risk.

AutoZone, Inc. (AZO) is a retailer and distributor of automotive replacement parts and accessories. In 2009, the company operated about 4,400 stores in the United States, Puerto Rico and Mexico. Each of its stores carries a product line for cars, sport utility vehicles, vans and light trucks, including new and remanufactured automotive hard parts, maintenance items, accessories and non-automotive products.

In exhibit 6.29 the EPS line shows the stellar growth that the company experienced throughout the last twenty years. In this case study, we examine AutoZone from April of 1999 until August of 2011. As you will see, there were not too many opportunities to buy the stock when valuations were considered to be at a low-risk level.

In exhibit 6.30 we begin in April 1999 by placing our buy target at $24.10, which is based on projecting the shape of the EPS line from

Exhibit 6.29 AutoZone (AZO, August 2011)

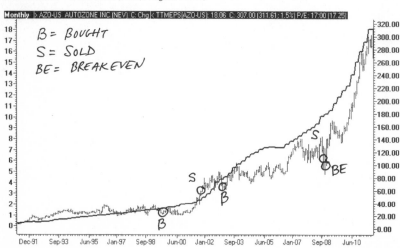

Exhibit 6.30   AutoZone (AZO, April 1999)

the previous low valuation when the shares traded around $20.50 in October 1998.

In exhibit 6.31 we raise our buy target to $25.10 because the EPS line has risen further. We then succeed in buying at $25.10 in August 1999 and the shares trade through our target and reach a low of $22.56 before recovering. We then place our sell target at $38.90 by projecting the shape of the EPS line off the high valuation of $37.31 in February 1999.

Exhibit 6.31   AutoZone (AZO, December 1999)

Exhibit 6.32 AutoZone (AZO, June 2000)

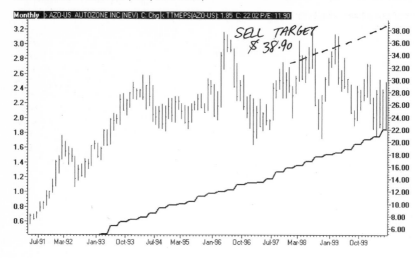

In exhibit 6.32 AutoZone trades slightly lower, so we patiently wait for the rising earnings to support the stock price and eventually push it higher. Note that this lower valuation would not be characterized as a valuation reset because the P/E ratio is 11.9×, compared to when we bought at $25.10 (exhibit 6.31) when the low valuation was reached at $22.56 and the P/E was 13.1×. A valuation reset is a noticeable and dramatic change in the valuation range.

In exhibit 6.33 we raise the selling target to $56.90 based on the evolving shape of the EPS line, and are able to sell at this price in October 2001. We then place our buy target at $44.10.

In exhibit 6.34, based on the evolving EPS line, we raise our buy target to $62.10 and manage to buy in January when the stock trades as low as $58.21. We set the sell target at $94.90. Note the accelerating growth in EPS. In a case like this, the valuation range usually begins to rise because the earnings stream will be expected to be much larger in the future. The acceleration in EPS growth is a sign that one can set more aggressive sell targets. In other words, it is likely that as long as the EPS is growing at a faster rate each quarter, investors will be willing to pay a higher multiple or valuation than at the previous high level.

Exhibit 6.33 AutoZone (AZO, December 2001)

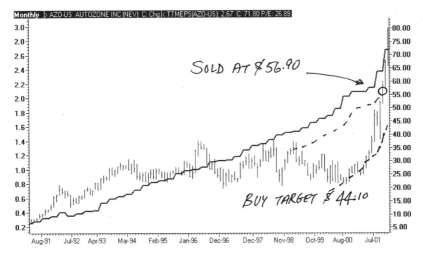

Exhibit 6.34 AutoZone (AZO, January 2003)

In exhibit 6.35 we raise the sell target to $108.90 because the EPS has risen. Note that the EPS is growing much more rapidly than in the period before 2001.

In exhibit 6.36 we raise the sell target again to $114.90 as the EPS continues to improve.

Exhibit 6.35 AutoZone (AZO, December 2003)

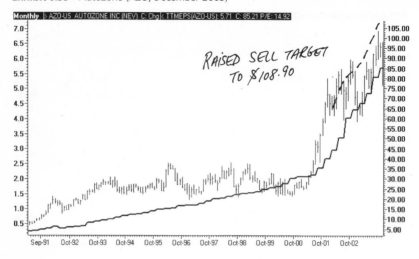

Exhibit 6.36 AutoZone (AZO, December 2004)

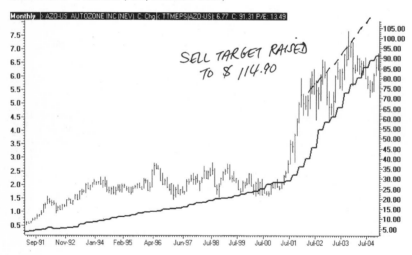

In exhibit 6.37, we see an unexpected decline in EPS so we reduce the sell target to $100.90. All things being normal, this change in EPS is a caution sign, so we begin to lower our expectations at this point.

In exhibit 6.38, AutoZone's EPS resumes its upward trend, but we sell at $102.90 because this is the high end of the valuation range that

Exhibit 6.37 AutoZone (AZO, December 2005)

Exhibit 6.38 AutoZone (AZO, December 2006)

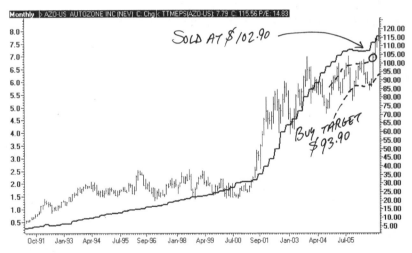

had been established earlier. Simultaneously, we set the new buy target at $93.90.

In exhibit 6.39 the EPS continues its upward trend and we raise our buy target to $102.10.

In exhibit 6.40 we buy at $116.10 based on what we perceive to be the low end of the valuation range, but then the stock drops to less than $100 per share and there is a valuation reset. Based on the valuation

Exhibit 6.39 AutoZone (AZO, December 2007)

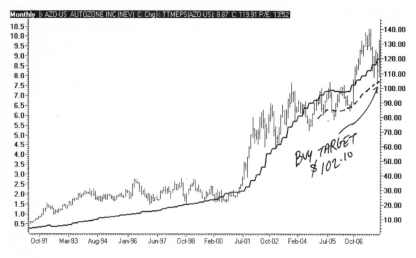

Exhibit 6.40 AutoZone (AZO, October 2008)

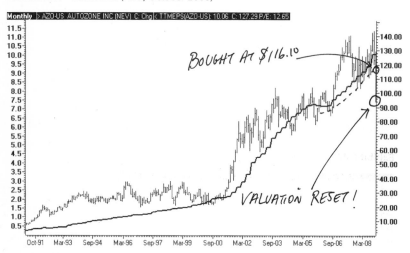

reset, we modify our sell target to break even at $116.10. Once we succeed in selling, we will look at the new valuation range and set a new buy target based on the lower valuation range.

In exhibit 6.41 we see that the stock drops all the way to $84.66 before reaching a bottom. The stock subsequently rises and we manage to sell at our break-even price of $116.10. This whipsawing occurred in the climax of the credit crisis, when investors were shaken by the unknown

Exhibit 6.41 AutoZone (AZO, January 2009)

repercussions of the crisis. The Purple Chips approach doesn't try to second-guess what will happen in a case like this; we have clear rules which state that if a valuation reset occurs, the best strategy is to sell at breakeven and re-enter at the low end of the new valuation range. In this case the new buy target is set at $102.10, which is slightly higher than the extreme low valuations that were seen during the sell-off.

In exhibit 6.42 the EPS continues its upward progression and we raise our buy target to $124.10. Note how the credit crisis affects the

Exhibit 6.42 AutoZone (AZO, December 2009)

Exhibit 6.43 AutoZone (AZO, December 2010)

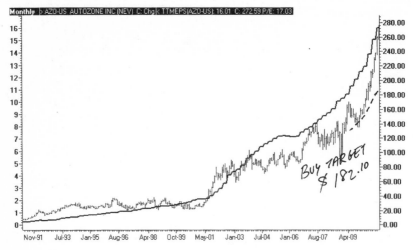

valuation of AutoZone in 2008 and 2009: The stock declines in price in spite of the unrelenting growth in EPS. These types of widespread valuation resets often create incredible opportunities for those investors who are objective in their analysis.

In exhibit 6.43, based on the evolution of EPS, we raise our buy target to $182.10.

In exhibit 6.44, based on the shape of the EPS line, we raise our buy target to $229.10.

Exhibit 6.44 AutoZone (AZO, August 2011)

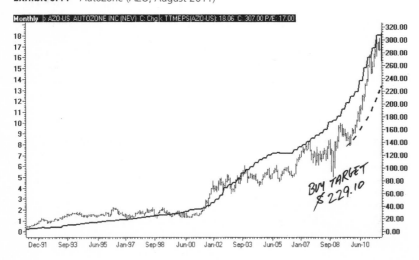

Exhibit 6.45 Purple Chips Results for AutoZone*

AutoZone				
Date	Buy	Date	Sell	Gain/Loss
July 1999	$ 25.10	Oct. 2001	$ 56.90	$31.80
Jan. 2003	$ 62.10	Oct. 2008	$102.90	$40.80
Nov. 2008	$116.10	Dec. 2008	$116.10	$ 0.00
			Total gain/loss	$72.60

*% of time period invested in stock (as of August 2011): 98 months/145 = 68%

In exhibit 6.45 we present a summary of the transactions that would have been made in AutoZone by following the Purple Chips methodology.

AutoZone Case Study Summary

To summarize the case study of AutoZone, we note the following points:

- Throughout the years that we examined, AutoZone had very fast growing earnings. This was reflected in the stellar progression of the stock price, but nevertheless the Purple Chips approach was able to identify a few opportunities when the stock was in the low end of its valuation range. I remind readers that this approach is based on identifying low-risk entry points, which can require extreme discipline and patience before an opportunity will present itself.
- Between 1999 and 2011 the price of AutoZone ranged from $25.10 to $310.87. In this case, the Purple Chips method captured $72.60 per share in profit.
- Following the Purple Chips approach meant that an investor had his capital invested for 98 months out of the 145 months in this study or for 68% of the time period covered.
- A stock market correction affects all stocks and can create once-in-a-decade buying opportunities.
- Using the trend in earnings as a reference point, investors can profit from price aberrations that are caused by fear and greed.

Case Study: Johnson & Johnson

In the following case study, we examine Johnson & Johnson (JNJ), one of the premier health care stocks that fits all of the criteria of Purple Chips. Johnson & Johnson engages in the research and development, manufacture and sale of various products in the health care field worldwide. The company operates in three segments: consumer, pharmaceutical and medical devices and diagnostics.

Exhibit 6.46 summarizes the transactions that the Purple Chips approach would have made on Johnson & Johnson between April 1999 and August 2011.

In exhibit 6.47 we begin in April 1999 and set our buy target at $34.10 by projecting the EPS line off the low valuation set back in late 1997. Note that at this time, the P/E ratio is hovering around 35×, which is much higher than the historical average P/E for the stock market. In a case such as this, a conservative entry point is recommended.

In exhibit 6.48, based on the evolution of the EPS, we raise the buy target to $36.10. Note that if we buy at $36.10, based on the EPS of $1.51, the P/E will be 23.9×.

Exhibit 6.46   Johnson & Johnson (JNJ, September 2011)

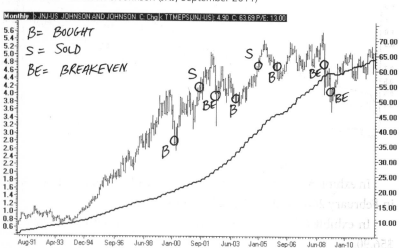

Exhibit 6.47 Johnson & Johnson (JNJ, April 1999)

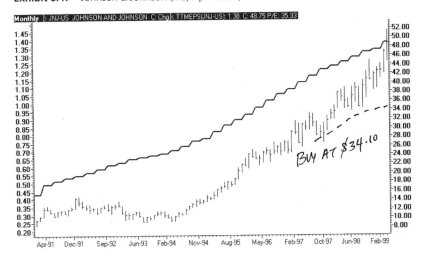

Exhibit 6.48 Johnson & Johnson (JNJ, January 2000)

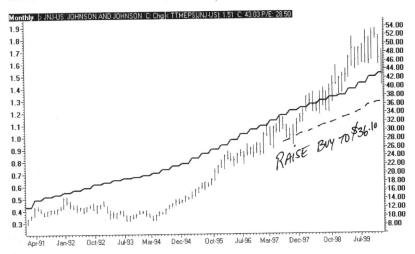

In exhibit 6.49, based on the shape of the EPS line, we buy at $36.10 in February 2000 and set the sell target at $54.90.

In exhibit 6.50, due to the rising EPS, we raise the sell target to $56.90.

Exhibit 6.49 Johnson & Johnson (JNJ, June 2000)

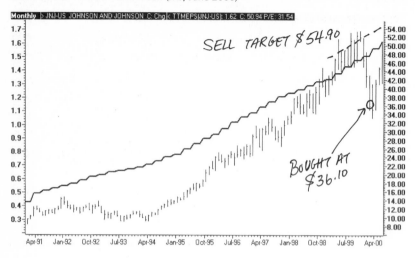

Exhibit 6.50 Johnson & Johnson (JNJ, December 2000)

In exhibit 6.51 we project the EPS line off the most recent high prices (between $50 and $52), which occurs between December 2000 and January 2001. This leads us to lower the sell target to $51.90.

In exhibit 6.52, based on the evolution of the EPS line, we raise the sell target and sell at $53.90 in June 2001. We then set the buy target at $48.10.

Exhibit 6.51   Johnson & Johnson (JNJ, March 2001)

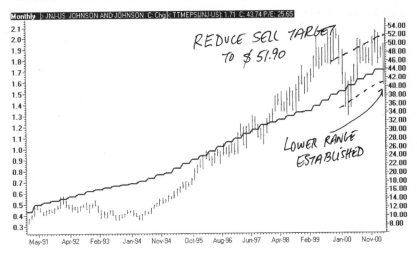

Exhibit 6.52   Johnson & Johnson (JNJ, December 2001)

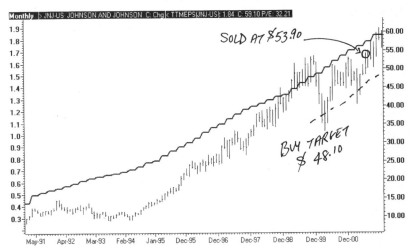

In exhibit 6.53, based on the shape of the EPS line, we raise the buy target to $52.10. Note that on the chart below, I did not draw the EPS line at the buy target of $52.10 because the last trade was at $52.26, therefore the EPS line is almost at the buy target.

In exhibit 6.54 we buy at $52.10 and then Johnson & Johnson experiences a valuation reset, so we follow the Purple Chips rule and

Exhibit 6.53   Johnson & Johnson (JNJ, June 2002)

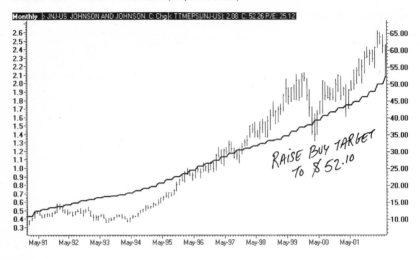

Exhibit 6.54   Johnson & Johnson (JNJ, December 2002)

sell shortly afterward at the break-even price of $52.10. We then set the new buy target at $46.10, which corresponds to the low end of the valuation range.

In exhibit 6.55 we raise the buy target to $51.10 based on the evolution of the EPS line. We then buy the stock in August. The sell target is set at $57.90.

Exhibit 6.55 Johnson & Johnson (JNJ, August 2003)

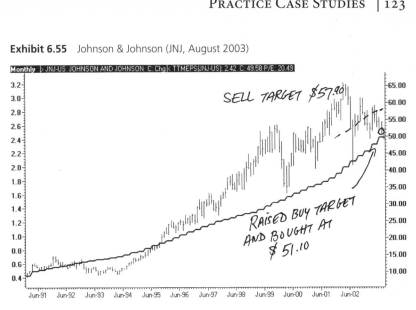

Exhibit 6.56 Johnson & Johnson (JNJ, June 2004)

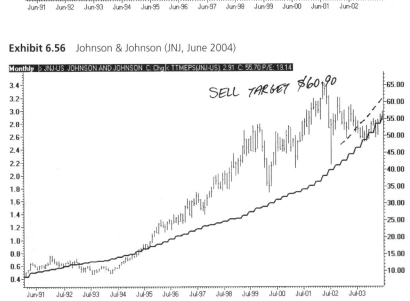

In exhibit 6.56 we raise the sell target to $60.90 because the EPS has been rising.

In exhibit 6.57 the sell target is set at $61.90 and the stock is sold in December 2004. At the same time, we set the new buy target at $58.10. This sell target was chosen because this was the upper end of the valuation range for Johnson & Johnson during the last year.

Exhibit 6.57 Johnson & Johnson (JNJ, December 2004)

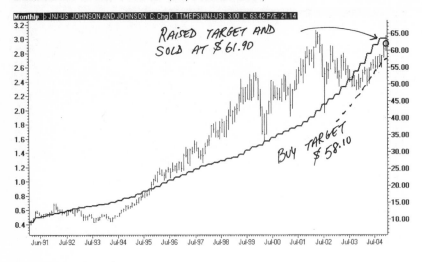

Exhibit 6.58 Johnson & Johnson (JNJ, December 2005)

In exhibit 6.58, based on the evolving EPS, we raise the buy target to $61.10 and set the sell target at $71.90. Note how the valuation of Johnson & Johnson has been declining since we began this case study. It now trades at a P/E of 17.5×, compared to the mid- to high 20s in 1999.

In exhibit 6.59 we raise the sell target to $71.90 based on the increasing EPS.

Exhibit 6.59   Johnson & Johnson (JNJ, December 2006)

In exhibit 6.60 we buy at $61.10 in October 2008. Johnson & Johnson experiences a valuation reset in November 2008 when its stock price falls to a low of $52.06. We then place a sell order to sell at breakeven and succeed in selling at $61.10. We set a buy target at $56.10 based on the new valuation range. Note that this period was the beginning of the credit crisis, during which many good stocks experienced valuation resets.

Exhibit 6.60   Johnson & Johnson (JNJ, November 2008)

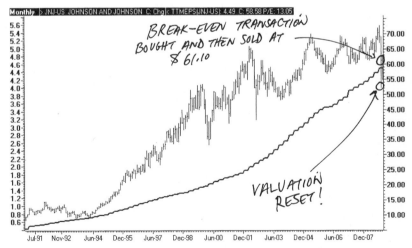

Exhibit 6.61 Johnson & Johnson (JNJ, June 2009)

In exhibit 6.61 we see that the credit crisis has caused a further valuation reset. We buy at $56.10 in December 2008. We then place a sell order to sell at breakeven because there is another valuation reset when the stock price falls to a low of $46.25 in March 2009. We manage to sell in May 2009 at our price. At this point, the new buy target is set at $51.10.

In exhibit 6.62 we raise the buy target to $52.10 because the EPS is increasing.

Exhibit 6.62 Johnson & Johnson (JNJ, June 2010)

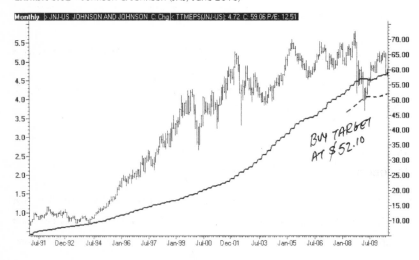

Exhibit 6.63   Johnson & Johnson (JNJ, September 2011)

Exhibit 6.64   Purple Chips Results for Johnson & Johnson*

Johnson & Johnson				
Date	Buy	Date	Sell	Gain/Loss
Feb. 2000	$36.10	June 2001	$53.90	$17.80
July 2002	$52.10	Aug. 2002	$52.10	$ 0.00
Aug. 2003	$51.10	Dec. 2004	$61.90	$10.80
Dec. 2005	$61.10	Nov. 2008	$61.10	$ 0.00
Jan. 2009	$56.10	May 2009	$56.10	$ 0.00
		Total gain/loss to date		$28.60

*% of time period invested in stock (as of August 2011): 75 months/138 = 54%

In exhibit 6.63 the EPS continues to rise so the buy target is raised to $57.10.

Exhibit 6.64 illustrates the transactions that occurred in Johnson & Johnson by applying the Purple Chips methodology.

Johnson & Johnson Case Study Summary

In conclusion we note the following points:

- As was the case with the most stocks, Johnson & Johnson was not able to avoid the tsunami of bad economic news that weighed on stocks in 2008 and 2009, so there were several break-even trades.

However, the Purple Chips approach still managed to identify a couple of low-risk entry points and was very successful because it managed to capture $28.60 of profit over the time period examined, yet the stock price increased by only $20 ($56.10 − $36.10 = $20). This illustrates how the Purple Chips approach can be superior to the traditionally passive buy and hold approach.

- The Purple Chips approach was invested in JNJ for 75 months out of 138 months studied or 54% of the time period covered.

Case Study: General Dynamics

In the following case study, we examine General Dynamics, one of the top Purple Chips in the defense industry. General Dynamics Corporation (GD) provides business aviation, combat vehicles, weapons systems and munitions, military and commercial shipbuilding, and communications and information technology products and services worldwide.

This case study shows how one must be extremely patient with some stocks, because low-risk opportunities may take years to materialize. Purple Chips is focused on finding low-risk entry points to buy great companies.

In exhibit 6.65, I show a summary of the buy and sell points that an investor would have made by following the Purple Chips model between June 2000 and September 2011.

In exhibit 6.66, we set the buy target at $22.10 by projecting the EPS line from the low valuations that were made in 1995.

In exhibit 6.67, the buy target is raised to $28.10 because of the increasing EPS.

In exhibit 6.68, we raise the buy target to $33.10 because of the increasing EPS. We buy when our price is reached in January. Based on the shape of the EPS line, we set the sell target at $47.90.

Exhibit 6.65   General Dynamics (GD, September 2011)

Exhibit 6.66   General Dynamics (GD, June 2000)

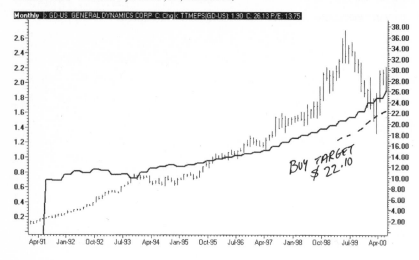

Exhibit 6.67   General Dynamics (GD, June 2000)

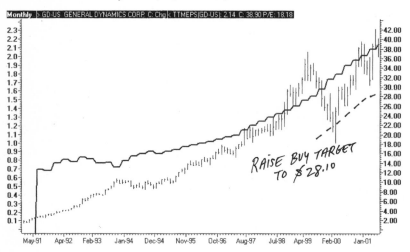

In exhibit 6.69, we see that General Dynamics has three consecutive quarters of declining EPS. Based on the Purple Chips rules, we know that this could be a harbinger of future problems; therefore we immediately sell at $37.79. Note that in this case the real sale price could have been higher, but the worst price was used to demonstrate the conservative nature of Purple Chips investing.

Exhibit 6.68 General Dynamics (GD, January 2003)

Exhibit 6.69 General Dynamics (GD, September 2003)

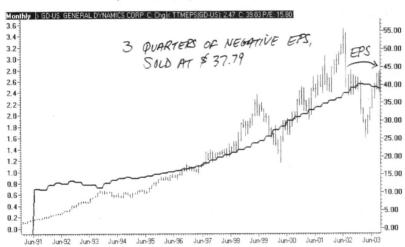

In exhibit 6.70, we see that the decline in EPS was just a short-term aberration as the EPS resumes its upward trend. We sold a year earlier, but will now set a buy target at $37.10 because the EPS is back on trend. It is better to be safe than sorry.

In exhibit 6.71 we raise the buy target to $46.10 because of the improvement in EPS.

Exhibit 6.70   General Dynamics (GD, September 2004)

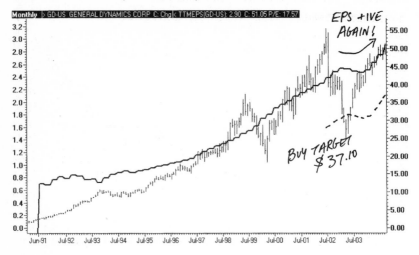

Exhibit 6.71   General Dynamics (GD, September 2004)

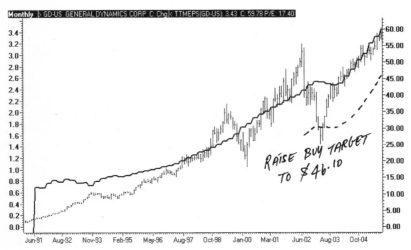

In exhibit 6.72 we raise the buy target to $69.10. Note how the stock of General Dynamics has been contained in a fairly narrow trading range for the last three years.

In exhibit 6.73, because of the increasing EPS, the buy target is raised to $73.10 and we buy in September. All things being normal, we would have set a sell target at around $97.90. Note that this is at

Exhibit 6.72   General Dynamics (GD, September 2007)

Exhibit 6.73   General Dynamics (GD, September 2008)

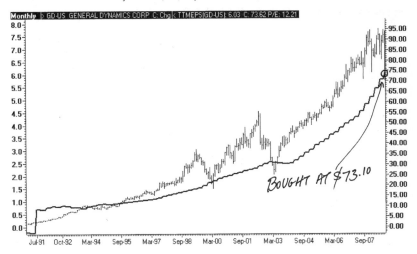

the beginning of the credit crisis, when all stocks succumbed to lower valuations as investors lost confidence.

In exhibit 6.74, the credit crisis takes hold and fear grips the stock market; lower valuations ensue. General Dynamics has a valuation reset when the stock price falls to $35.28 in March of 2009 and we place an order to sell at the break-even price of $73.10. Note that

Exhibit 6.74   General Dynamics (GD, June 2009)

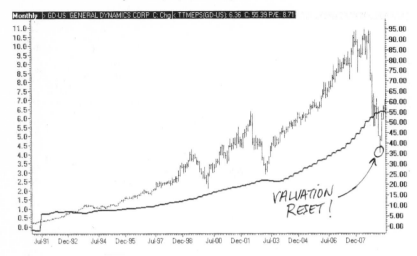

Exhibit 6.75   General Dynamics (GD, June 2010)

we do not establish a new buy target until we have exited our current position.

In exhibit 6.75 we sell at the break-even price of $73.10 in February 2010. Only then do we set the buy target at $52.10. Note that the EPS has two consecutive quarters of decline and then begins rising again. The Purple Chips rule is to sell only if there are three consecutive quarters of declining EPS.

Exhibit 6.76   General Dynamics (GD, June 2011)

In exhibit 6.76, based on the rising EPS, we raise the buy target to
$60.10.

In exhibit 6.77 we buy at $60.10 in August 2011 and place a sell
target at $75.90 by projecting the shape of the EPS line from the most
recent high valuations, which were seen in March 2011.

Exhibit 6.77   General Dynamics (GD, September 2011)

Exhibit 6.78 Purple Chips Results for General Dynamics*

General Dynamics				
Date	Buy	Date	Sell	Gain/Loss
Jan. 2003	$33.10	Sept. 2003	$37.79	$4.69
Sept. 2008	$73.10	Feb. 2010	$73.10	$0.00
Sept. 2011	$60.10	?**	?**	?**
			Total gain/loss to date	$ 4.69

*% of time period invested in stock (as of September 2011): 27 months/105 = 26%.

**The question marks (?) indicate that the transaction had not been closed by September 2011.

In exhibit 6.78 we recap the transactions in General Dynamics.

General Dynamics Case Study Summary
Conclusion:

- This case study was a good example of a stock that remained expensive for years until it finally presented a buying opportunity after the crash of 2008-2009. General Dynamics was not a very volatile stock and consequently there were not many instances where the Purple Chips approach could identify low-valuation entry points.
- As I've mentioned previously, it takes time and patience to make profits. Several years can pass before a Purple Chip reaches a low-risk valuation.
- Stock market crashes are anomalies and are difficult to predict. It is better to invest by applying sound principles such as buying a stock because it's undervalued than to stay out of the market due to the fear that a crash may occur or continue. If investors avoid the stock market for fear of a crash, they will always miss out on major buying opportunities. In the words of Warren Buffett: "Big opportunities come infrequently. When it's raining gold, reach for a bucket, not a thimble."

Next, we wrap up with a summary of the reasons why investing in Purple Chips makes sense.

CHAPTER 7

PURPLE CHIPS SUMMARIZED

In this chapter, I summarize the fundamentals of the Purple Chips approach that will help you become a more successful investor.

1. **Tune out the noise:** The media has the unfortunate habit of distracting investors by focusing on the latest flavor-of-the-day hot stocks. Purple Chips cuts through the noise and lets you focus on the highest-quality investments at the best valuations.

2. **Invest like the best:** The Purple Chips approach emulates the Warren Buffett style of buying great companies at good prices. The big difference is that Purple Chips recognizes when these companies are at high valuations, so that it can sell them and then buy them again when they are at reasonable valuations.

3. **Best of class:** Many of the stocks that show up in the Purple Chips model will appear on "best of" lists: best dividend growers, best earnings growth, best financial health, lowest price to book and best employer. They are the "best of class" companies.

4. **Buy low and sell high:** One of the most gratifying results of Purple Chips is selling at a high valuation, realizing a profit and then repurchasing in the same great company at a low valuation.

5. **Recycle your profits:** Purple Chips is a life saver in a sideways to lower market because it tells you when to sell. It is not just a buy and hold strategy. It is a buy, hold, sell and buy again strategy.

6. **High quality = superior returns:** As was mentioned in Chapter 2, this is proven when you consider that if you bought each of the top twenty-five Purple Chips at the highest price prior to the crash of 2008 and 2009, the basket of top Purple Chips performed 22% better (excluding the benefit of dividends) than the S&P 500 Average over the same time period![1]

7. **Simple is better:** Purple Chips puts professional analysis within reach of the average investor. This method allows any investor to analyze a company by making a quick visual inspection of the long-term graph of price and EPS.

8. **Small steps = big gains:** Most wealth is created through a lifetime of small actions rather than a few big ones. Purple Chips embodies this philosophy by taking profits when valuations are high instead of going for the rare home run.

9. **Comprehensive plan:** Purple Chips is a comprehensive approach that has all of the elements of a well-founded plan—it considers quality and gives entry and exit points if the plan works or doesn't work.

10. **Show your children:** Teach your children the Purple Chips method and they will always have money.

11. **Character flaws:** Companies are living organisms that are governed by people. Purple Chips helps you spot the flaws and avoid the mistakes that are made by the people who run the companies.

12. **Valuation is a dynamic process:** Most investors are misled into looking at price without considering earnings. Both must be examined together if an investor wants to gauge value.

Endnotes

Chapter 1

1. Much of the pre-2008 data is based on back testing. Back testing is when you go back in time and apply a set of assumptions to a data series. Note that some of the transactions were performed by the author.

Chapter 2

1. Ibbotson Associates 2008 Yearbook.

2. Ned Davis Research 2009.

3. For a current list of Purple Chips, please go to www.purplechips.com.

Chapter 3

1. In August 2011, there were 245 companies listed on U.S. stock markets that met the criteria of the Purple Chips model. See www.purplechips.com for the current list of Purple Chip stocks.

Chapter 4

1. The current E (earnings) of the P/E figure for the S&P 500 Index can be found on the Standard & Poors website at www.standardandpoors.com.

2. Economist and author Robert Shiller has written extensively on the subject of market valuation and expected returns. See http://www.econ.yale.

edu/~shiller/. See also John Hussman for some excellent articles on this subject: http://www.hussmanfunds.com/researchInsight.html.

3. As of August 2011, valuations for Abbott Labs were still trending lower.

4. John Mauldin, "The Dark Side of Deficits," August 27, 2010; http://www.johnmauldin.com/images/uploads/pdf/mwo082710.pdf.

5. Pu Shen, "The PE Ratio and Stock Market Performance," 4th Quarter 2000, Federal Reserve Bank of Kansas City.

6. Ed Easterling, "The PE Report," October 1, 2011, Crestmont Research.

7. Burton Malkiel, *A Random Walk Down Wall Street* (New York: W.W. Norton, 2007).

Chapter 5

1. For the latest EPS numbers of a Purple Chip stock, ask your financial professional or go to www.purplechips.com.

Chapter 7

1. The time period used to compare the S&P 500 Index to the basket of Purple Chips was from October 2007, when the index was at it's highest at $1576.09, to July 7, 2011, when the index was at $1353.22.

Index

Page numbers in *italics* indicate charts.

John Schwinghamer is a Portfolio Manager with Scotia MacLeod in Montreal. He started his career in investments in 1984 as floor trader at the Montreal Exchange and then became a stockbroker and an expert in derivatives. John has also held management and partnership positions in several investment firms, and he currently manages the portfolios of a select group of high net worth clients. He has a Bachelor of Commerce in finance from Concordia University, as well as extensive securities industry accreditation. Since 2003, he has been a lead judge for the International Case Competition at the John Molson School of Business at his alma mater. He has also been an expert witness in derivatives court cases. John lives in Montreal with his wife and their two children.

Notes

Notes

Notes

Notes